Authentic Leadership in Schools

This compelling book explores how school leaders can build trust, embrace authenticity and lead in a way that feels genuinely aligned with their values, while achieving their desired outcomes. Drawing on Evelyn Forde's extensive experience in school leadership and the latest research, it highlights how authentic leadership fosters an inclusive school culture where both staff and students can thrive.

Rooted in the realities of school leadership – such as inspection pressures, workforce challenges and the growing demands on emotional and ethical capacity – the book offers practical guidance on acting with clarity and integrity amidst competing priorities and uncertainty. With an emphasis on shaping cultures through behaviour, communication and the effective handling of disagreement, the chapters explore:

- Using vision and values to establish priorities and drive positive change.
- Fostering an inclusive culture where every voice is heard.
- Leading authentically in challenging situations.
- Delegating effectively and building trust.
- Holding people to account and navigating difficult conversations.

Featuring real-world examples and an opportunity for reflective commentary, this essential read is perfect for current and aspiring school leaders who want to lead with integrity, authenticity and create healthy, harmonious and happy teams.

Evelyn Forde, MBE, is a former President of the Association of School and College Leaders (ASCL) and an esteemed headteacher. Recognised for her outstanding contributions to education, particularly in promoting diversity and inclusion in schools, Evelyn was awarded an MBE for her services to education. After concluding her tenure in formal leadership roles, she remains actively involved in the education sector, providing consultancy services to schools and educational bodies on issues of leadership, equity and school improvement strategies.

Authentic Leadership in Schools

How to Win Hearts and Minds

Evelyn Forde

Routledge
Taylor & Francis Group
LONDON AND NEW YORK

Designed cover image: © Getty Images

First published 2027
by Routledge
4 Park Square, Milton Park, Abingdon, Oxon OX14 4RN

and by Routledge
605 Third Avenue, New York, NY 10158

Routledge is an imprint of the Taylor & Francis Group, an informa business

British Library Cataloguing-in-Publication Data
A catalogue record for this book is available from the British Library

Library of Congress Cataloging-in-Publication Data
Names: Forde, Evelyn (Headteacher) author
Title: Authentic leadership : how to win hearts and minds / Evelyn Forde.
Description: Abingdon, Oxon ; New York, NY : Routledge, 2026. | Includes bibliographical references and index. | Identifiers: LCCN 2026016914 (print) | LCCN 2026016915 (ebook) | ISBN 9781041064909 hardback | ISBN 9781041064893 paperback | ISBN 9781003635666 ebook
Subjects: LCSH: Educational leadership | School management and organization
Classification: LCC LB2805 .F6155 2026 (print) | LCC LB2805 (ebook)
LC record available at https://lccn.loc.gov/2026016914
LC ebook record available at https://lccn.loc.gov/2026016915

ISBN: 978-1-041-06490-9 (hbk)
ISBN: 978-1-041-06489-3 (pbk)
ISBN: 978-1-003-63566-6 (ebk)

DOI: 10.4324/9781003635666

Typeset in Melior
by KnowledgeWorks Global Ltd.

"Evelyn Forde stands out for me as a leader. *Brave* in her drive for justice in a society where there are unlevel playfields. *Uncompromising* – in her passion, commitment and drive to ensure there is equity for all. *Authentic* in what she does, how she acts and who she champions".

John Murphy, *Education Leadership Mentor, Advisor & Public Speaker*

"Evelyn epitomises values-led leadership in action, whether leading schools or spearheading initiatives that increase diverse representation in education. In her authentic style, she is that rare phenomenon: an integrous leader fully committed to transforming organisations and society with lasting, measurable change. This is a superb book from a remarkable woman. Courageous and timely, it is a must-read that will be invaluable in any leader's toolkit".

Michelle Moore, *Global Speaker*

"Evelyn makes her argument with clarity and wisdom. Her integrity, and considered demand for better practice, is irresistible".

Sinead McBrearty, *Chief Executive Officer at Education Support*

"There are very few leadership books that tell the truth without shouting. This is one of them.

What Evelyn Forde offers here is not a new framework or a polished theory of leadership. It is something far more powerful and far more needed: an honest reckoning with what it means to lead human beings, in complex systems, with integrity intact.

At the heart of this book is a simple but radical proposition: that belonging is not a programme, a policy or a box to be ticked, but a leadership responsibility. Evelyn reminds us that culture is shaped not by what leaders say they value, but by what people experience every day in how decisions are made, how mistakes are handled, how power is exercised and how dignity is protected.

This is values-led leadership in its truest form. Leadership that understands that standards and care are not opposites. That accountability does not require fear. That people can only give their best in environments where they feel seen, safe and able to bring their whole selves to the table.

What struck me most is the moral clarity running through these pages. Evelyn is unapologetic in naming the emotional labour carried by staff, the quiet erosion that happens when voices are ignored, and the profound difference it makes when leaders choose repair over defensiveness, humility over ego, humanity over hierarchy. This is leadership that does not hide behind systems, but takes responsibility for how those systems land on real people.

As someone who has spent decades working across civil society, education and global youth leadership, I know that trust is the currency that determines whether institutions endure or erode. Trust is built when leaders are consistent, self-aware and willing to be honest about both their power and their limitations. Evelyn writes from lived experience, not abstraction, and it shows. Her reflections on authenticity, imposter syndrome and the courage to lead as yourself will resonate with anyone who has ever felt they had to contort themselves to fit a leadership mould that was never designed for them.

This book speaks directly to the moment we are in. A moment where traditional command-and-control models are no longer sufficient. Where people are asking not just for competence, but for conscience. Not just for vision, but for values. Not just for leaders who can drive outcomes, but for leaders who can hold people with care while doing so.

Belonging, as Evelyn so powerfully shows, is the foundation from which becoming is possible. When people feel they belong, they take risks, they lead, they stay, they grow. That is true in schools, in organisations, and in society more broadly. Cultures of belonging do not happen by accident. They are created, sustained and protected by leaders who understand that how we lead matters just as much as what we achieve.

This is a book for leaders who are prepared to look inward as well as outward. For those who understand that authentic leadership is not performative, but deeply relational. And for those who believe, as I do, that the most lasting legacies are built not through control, but through trust, integrity and humanity".

Dr. Tessy Ojo, CBE, *Chief Executive Officer, The Diana Award*

Contents

Acknowledgements

This book would not exist without the people who have shaped my thinking, challenged my assumptions and supported me throughout my leadership journey.

First and foremost, I want to thank the colleagues, leaders and communities I have worked alongside over the years. You trusted me with your stories, your frustrations, your hopes and your courage. Much of what is explored in these pages has been shaped by conversations held in offices, classrooms, corridors and quiet moments after long days. I am deeply grateful for your honesty and your willingness to reflect on what leadership looks like in practice, not just in principle.

My sincere thanks go to the leaders who generously contributed their reflections to this book: **Nav Sanghara, Elroy Aidouni-Cahill** and **Sufian Sadiq**. Their stories are thoughtful, grounded and deeply human. Reading their reflections gives me genuine hope for the future of leadership in education and reassurance that our children are, and will continue to be, in safe hands. Their contributions remind us that authentic leadership is alive, practised and evolving in real contexts every day.

I am also particularly grateful to **Manny Botwe**, whose reflective account of leadership, voice and belonging adds a powerful and timely dimension to this book. His willingness to share a moment of challenge with such clarity and integrity exemplifies the courage and moral responsibility explored throughout these chapters.

I would like to thank **Geoff Barton, CBE**, for agreeing to write the foreword. His longstanding contribution to education and his commitment to thoughtful, values-led leadership have been influential to many, myself included. I am also grateful to those who have endorsed this book and supported its publication; your encouragement and belief in the importance of this work have meant a great deal.

There are individuals who have shaped my leadership long before this book was imagined, mentors, coaches and colleagues who asked difficult questions, offered perspective when it was needed and reminded me to return to what mattered most. Your influence is woven throughout these pages, even when unnamed.

I also want to acknowledge the teachers, support staff, governors and leaders who continue to work with care and commitment in increasingly complex and demanding contexts. This book is written with deep respect for the emotional labour and moral responsibility that leadership in education carries.

On a personal note, I am grateful to those closest to me who have supported this work in ways that are less visible but no less significant. Thank you for your patience, encouragement and understanding during the long hours of thinking, writing, revising and doubting.

Finally, I want to thank the readers of this book. If you have found yourself reflected in these pages, I hope you feel seen rather than judged. My hope is that this book offers not answers, but companionship and clarity as you navigate your own leadership journey.

Foreword

This is emphatically my kind of book about leadership and, specifically, about educational leadership. It's eminently readable, grounded, thought-provoking and ... exudes authenticity.

It's a book that has no swagger, no simplistic copy-and-paste solutions, no covert message that because I am a leader I should feel more important than you – the people I lead.

Instead, we are reminded that as educational leaders, whatever our role, we are engaged in a collective endeavour to improve the life-chances of children and young people, whatever their backgrounds.

And for Evelyn Forde, that moral purpose is palpable. As is humility.

Authentic Leadership is a book in which the sheer humanity of great leadership is moved centre-stage, frequently exploring the often-unnerving messiness of leading others, and powerfully acknowledging that, yes, sometimes some ideas work ... and then sometimes they don't.

This isn't textbook leadership. There aren't quick fixes. Instead, it is a compelling reflection about authentic, interpersonal leadership.

Anyone who has worked with Evelyn Forde – as I was privileged to do in my years as General Secretary of the Association of School & College Leaders – will recognise how Evelyn lives and breathes this approach. And, throughout her writing, they will recognise her distinctive voice.

Because Evelyn's story is itself a notable and often unexpected one. She hasn't traversed the usual routes into school-based – and then national – leadership. Hers has been a journey of adversity, challenges, constant learning and achievement.

And Evelyn Forde's Authentic Leadership totally gets that blend of introspective and public leadership. We worry inside whilst we aim to project confidence to the wider public. Such is leadership.

That's what Evelyn writes about so well – combining personal history, wide reading, leadership insights and a powerful moral compass. It's all done in a spirit of extraordinary professional generosity.

I commend this book to anyone working in schools or colleges, or anyone contemplating doing so. We are reminded that taking on responsibility for the next generation of young people, and for leading the adults who will help to shape them, is perhaps one of the most important roles society has.

And the kind of leadership required in these turbulent times is utterly and compellingly authentic.

Geoff Barton, CBE, Former English teacher, Headteacher, and General Secretary of the Association of School & College Leaders

Author's note

This book was not written from a place of certainty.

It was written from within the lived complexity of leadership, shaped by competing demands, responsibility for others and the ongoing work of acting with integrity when answers are unclear. Like many leaders, I searched for models and frameworks that promised clarity or control. What I learned instead is that leadership is less about certainty and more about judgement and less about performance and more about alignment.

Authentic leadership is frequently discussed, but less often examined honestly. In practice, it is disciplined and demanding. It asks leaders to act with clarity, to hold boundaries with compassion, and to stay in difficult conversations even when avoidance would be easier. It requires attention not only to what we do, but to how and why we do it.

Throughout this book, I draw on my own leadership journey, alongside the experiences of others, not to offer a template or prescription, but to surface patterns, tensions and choices that many leaders will recognise. The reflections included at the end of each chapter are designed to slow you down, not to add to your workload. They are prompts to notice what is already present in your leadership practice, and to consider what might need greater attention.

This book is not neutral. It is grounded in a belief that leadership carries moral weight, that how leaders behave matters, and that cultures are shaped as much by what is tolerated as by what is stated. It assumes that leadership is relational, that trust and belonging are not optional extras and that accountability can be exercised with humanity.

You do not need to agree with everything in these pages. My hope is that this book helps you think more clearly about how you choose to lead, particularly when the work is hard. If it leaves you slightly unsettled at times, that may be a sign it is doing its work.

Above all, this book is an invitation. An invitation to pause, to reflect and to lead with intention. Not perfectly, but honestly. Not alone, but in relationship with others.

How to use this book

This book is not designed to be rushed.

While it can be read from start to finish, it is written to be engaged with deliberately and, at times, slowly. The chapters build on one another, but each also stands alone, allowing you to return to particular themes or moments that feel most relevant to your leadership context.

You may notice that the book moves between analysis, lived experience and reflection. This is intentional. Leadership is rarely linear, and the challenges leaders face cannot always be resolved through strategy alone. At points, you may recognise your own experiences in the examples shared; at others, you may feel prompted to pause and consider how your leadership shows up in quieter, less visible ways.

At the end of each chapter, you will find a reflection section. These reflections are not tasks to be completed or questions to be answered perfectly. They are invitations to notice patterns, behaviours and assumptions that shape how you lead. You may choose to engage with them privately, to journal responses or to use them as prompts for coaching, supervision or leadership development conversations. There is no expectation that every reflection will feel immediately relevant; some may resonate more strongly at different points in your leadership journey.

You may also find it helpful to revisit certain chapters as your role or context changes. Leadership is shaped by timing as much as by intention, and what feels distant or theoretical at one moment may become immediate and practical at another. This book is designed to be returned to, not consumed once and set aside.

For those leading teams, schools or trusts, the chapters and reflections can also be used collectively. They may provide a shared language for discussing values, trust, accountability and belonging, or offer a starting point for conversations that feel difficult to initiate. Used in this way, the book becomes less about individual insight and more about collective understanding.

It is worth saying that this book does not offer a single model of authentic leadership. There are no checklists to follow or formulas to apply. Instead, it asks you to exercise judgement, to reflect honestly and to remain attentive to the impact of your leadership on others. You may agree with some perspectives and question others. Both responses are welcome.

If at any point you feel the urge to move quickly through a chapter, that may be a sign to pause. Authentic leadership often requires slowing down, especially in systems that reward speed and certainty. The space between chapters is as important as the chapters themselves.

Above all, use this book in a way that serves you and the people you lead. Dip in and out. Read alone or with others. Reflect now and return later. The work of authentic leadership is ongoing, and this book is intended to accompany you, not instruct you.

1 Introduction

Authentic leadership: How to win hearts and minds

Leadership can mean different things to different people. In schools, it is often associated with a badge – the title you receive upon becoming a middle or senior leader. But I start from a different premise altogether: if you work with and for young people, you are already a leader.

Every adult in a school shapes lives. Pupils watch how you show up, how you speak to others, how you respond under pressure and how you treat those with less power than you. Leadership is not confined to job titles or organisational charts; it lives in the everyday interactions that quietly shape culture, confidence and belonging.

Are leaders born or made? What type of leader are you? Which leadership style do you default to? These questions are often well-intentioned, yet they can also make leadership feel increasingly complex and, for some, unattainable. At a time when our schools need more leaders than ever, I want to challenge the idea that success depends on fitting a particular leadership mould.

Becoming a leader without realising it

When I began my career as a History teacher in North London in 1999, I didn't think of myself as a leader at all. I was focused on my craft, planning lessons, understanding my pupils and doing the best job I could in front of a class. The freedom of being an Newly Qualified Teacher (NQT) allowed me to be myself, but I was largely oblivious to the leadership ladder ahead of me or what it might take to climb it.

Only later did I realise something important: careers in education are rarely linear. Many of us take left and right turns because opportunities aren't available, don't feel right or arrive at the wrong time. Leadership often finds us before we feel ready for it.

DOI: 10.4324/9781003635666-1

That sense of not quite belonging in leadership spaces is something I hear repeatedly from aspiring leaders, particularly those stepping into responsibility before they feel ready.

At around year 3 of my headship, I realised I didn't need to become someone else to lead well. I just needed to be myself because everyone else was already taken. That realisation sits at the heart of what I mean by authentic leadership: accepting who you are, recognising the uniqueness you bring, and leading from that place with integrity. Anything else is exhausting, unsustainable and ultimately disengaging for both leaders and those they serve.

What do we mean by authentic leadership?

Authentic leadership can mean many things to many people. For me, it is about leading with integrity, transparency and empathy, particularly when the pressure is high and the decisions are uncomfortable.

Researchers Kernis and Goldman describe authenticity as resting on four key components: self-awareness, unbiased processing, values-aligned behaviour, and relational honesty (Kernis & Goldman, 2006). These ideas resonate deeply with school leadership, where relationships are not a 'soft' extra, but the bedrock of culture, trust and improvement.

Authenticity, however, is not about saying whatever you think or wearing your emotions on display at all times. It is a disciplined way of leading, one that requires reflection, courage and consistency. It asks leaders to align their values with their actions, even when no one is watching.

This book is written for leaders who want to lead in that way, not perfectly, but honestly.

Why authentic leadership matters now

We are leading in fragile times. Political uncertainty, social division and economic pressures are shaping the lives of the children and adults who walk into our schools every day. In that context, schools are expected to be places of safety, belonging and growth, not just academically but emotionally and socially too.

Traditional models of leadership built on control, compliance and authority alone are no longer sufficient. Young people, staff and communities are looking for leaders they can trust, leaders who are human, values-driven and prepared to listen.

From education to global movements, lasting change has always been driven by leaders who understand that relationships are not secondary to results; they are how results are achieved.

If you want a simple illustration of this, watch Rita Pierson's *Everybody Needs a Champion*. It became my go-to video for INSET days as a headteacher because it captures, in just a few minutes, what authentic leadership feels like in practice (Pierson, 2013).

Why this book, and why me?

This book draws on my lived experience of leading schools in challenging contexts, navigating systems that were not always designed with people like me in mind, and learning sometimes the hard way what it means to lead with authenticity.

I will share moments of success and moments of failure. I will explore how trust is built, how teams are formed, how difficult conversations are handled with dignity and how values show up not in mission statements, but in daily decisions.

You'll find practical strategies alongside reflective prompts, because authentic leadership is not something you read about once and master. It is a continual practice.

Whether you are an aspiring leader, a newly appointed leader, or someone who has carried the responsibility for years, I hope that this book will reassure you of one thing: you do not need to become someone else to lead well.

Where my story began?

When I was riding the number 8 bus to Oxford Street after truancy from secondary school, leadership was the last thing on my mind. No one noticed my absence. No one asked why I wasn't there.

Years later, after becoming a parent and returning to education, I encountered leaders who did the opposite: they saw me, invested time and believed in my potential. Those moments of being noticed, supported and challenged became the foundation of my leadership values.

Throughout this book, I return to the idea that leadership is not about position, but presence. It is about how we make others feel in our presence, and the impact that remains long after we've left the room.

An Invitation

This book is an invitation to reflect, to challenge yourself and to lead with intention. It is not a checklist or a leadership formula. It is a companion for leaders who want to win hearts and minds, not through charisma or authority, but through authenticity.

As you read on, I invite you to pause occasionally and look inward.

Reflection 1

- Who were the first leaders who had an impact on your life?
- What characteristics made them memorable?
- How have those experiences shaped your own leadership approach?

In this context, psychological safety is no longer a 'nice to have'. It is essential, not only for students, but for staff and leaders themselves. Where fear dominates, people retreat. Where trust is present, people stay, contribute and grow (Edmondson, 2018).

This is why authentic leadership matters now. Not because leaders have all the answers, but because honesty, humility and steadiness have become stabilising forces in uncertain systems.

In the chapters that follow, we will explore belonging, values, team culture, necessary conversations and what authentic leadership looks like in practice, especially when the stakes are high and the answers are unclear.

This is where the real work begins.

References

Kernis, M.H., & Goldman, B.M. (2006). A multicomponent conceptualization of authenticity. *Journal of Personality, 74*(4), 1068–1089.

Pierson, R. (2013). Every child needs a champion TED Talk. TED Conferences. https://www.ted.com/talks/rita_pierson_every_child_needs_a_champion

Edmondson, A. (2018). *The fearless organization: Creating psychological safety in the workplace for learning, innovation, and growth*. Wiley.

2 Why now? Leading with authenticity in uncertain times

The world feels fragile. Education sits at the intersection of political uncertainty, social division and economic constraint, and schools are carrying pressures that extend far beyond teaching and learning alone. For leaders, the question is no longer simply *how* to lead, but *why now*. Why does authentic, values-driven leadership matter more in this moment than at any other?

This chapter invites you to pause and reflect on the system you are leading within, the culture you are shaping and the kind of leader you are becoming. It speaks both to those already carrying responsibility and to those considering stepping into leadership, or even into the profession itself. It offers no illusion that the work is easy. But it does argue that how we lead now matters profoundly for staff, for students and for the long-term health of education itself.

To understand why this moment feels so charged, it helps to look back.

Learning from the past: The national challenge era

During my early years of teaching, the National Challenge was introduced with a clear and unapologetic ambition: to raise standards in struggling schools and create a more equitable education system. As both a teacher and a parent and as someone shaped by the education system myself, I welcomed the clarity of that moral purpose.

The London Challenge, in particular, represented something rare in education policy: sustained investment, collaboration over competition and trust in professional judgement. Schools were not positioned as failures, but as places of possibility. Leaders were encouraged to work together, not perform for inspection. Teachers felt valued, supported and part of something bigger than their own classrooms.

At its heart, the National Challenge rested on a simple but powerful belief: every child deserved access to effective leadership, excellent teaching and a school culture built on aspiration rather than deficit. Leadership mattered, not as an abstract concept, but as the engine of improvement.

DOI: 10.4324/9781003635666-2

What distinguished this period was not only the scale of funding or the structural reforms, but the tone. The language of improvement was relational rather than punitive. Schools were supported to lead change themselves, drawing on collaboration, shared responsibility and local knowledge. Moral purpose was not a slogan; it was enacted through relationships.

Looking back, it is easy to feel nostalgic. But this is not about romanticising the past. It is about recognising what happens when a system creates the conditions for leaders to lead authentically with trust, clarity and purpose rather than through fear, fragmentation or relentless compliance.

That contrast matters now more than ever.

Why this moment feels different?

Today's leaders are operating in a far more volatile environment. Policy shifts arrive with little notice. Accountability feels sharper and less forgiving. Resources are stretched. Public scrutiny is constant, and the emotional and moral load carried by school leaders has intensified.

And yet, the core truth remains unchanged: systems improve when leadership is grounded in integrity, relationships and moral purpose. When those conditions erode, authenticity becomes harder to sustain but also more necessary.

This is why 'why now' is not a rhetorical question. It is a leadership one.

Learning from the past: Leadership, systemness and moral purpose

Many esteemed and great leaders were involved in leading and delivering the strategy for the London Challenge and thereafter the National Challenge. To deepen my own reflection on what made the London Challenge and the National Challenge so powerful, I spoke to Steve Munby, former Chief Executive of the National College for School Leadership, whose influence on leadership development during that period was profound.

Steve is careful to clarify his role. The National College did not 'run' the London Challenge; rather, it played a crucial role in enabling school-to-school support. The College identified headteachers with the capacity and credibility to support other schools, trained them as consultant leaders and brokered relationships that were deliberately relational, not transactional. What mattered most was not imposing solutions but ensuring that *relationships worked*. If a partnership wasn't right, it was changed. That flexibility alone signalled a deep respect for professional judgement.

Yet the wider success of the London Challenge, Steve explains, lay in something more expansive: a sense of systemness. Under Tim Brighouse's leadership, London was framed not as a collection of competing schools, but as a shared moral project. Leaders were encouraged to see their responsibility as extending beyond their own gates. Language mattered. Schools were not labelled as failing, but as 'keys to success' schools. Opportunity replaced deficit. Belonging replaced blame.

Steve describes how Tim Brighouse visited every London school, creating a tangible connection between leaders and the centre. Teachers and headteachers felt seen, valued and part of something bigger. Behind it all sat a clear moral purpose: *every child in London mattered*. This wasn't rhetoric; it was enacted through relationships, collaboration and trust.

That same philosophy underpinned the National College's later work on system leadership, particularly through the creation of National Leaders of Education. At the time, school improvement often relied on advisers or, in extreme cases, replacing headteachers. What the College recognised was that many of the most effective leaders were unwilling to abandon their own schools to rescue others, and understandably so. The alternative was elegant: enable strong schools to support others *without leaving their own communities behind*.

Crucially, this work was never intended to be about empire-building. As Steve puts it, 'At the heart of it, for most people, was moral purpose'. The data bore this out. Schools supporting others improved. Schools being supported changed too. It was a rare win-win, built not on coercion, but on authentic leadership and shared responsibility.

Authenticity, Steve argues, was not incidental to this success; it was foundational. Leaders entering another school had to be trusted. If their presence felt performative, ego-driven or like a takeover, the work simply failed. 'The only way it really worked was to be authentic', he reflects. Without that, leaders were rejected, however strong their technical expertise.

Why authenticity was foundational, not optional?

This emphasis on authenticity was not accidental. Steve is clear that the National College explicitly foregrounded moral purpose and authentic leadership in its programmes, conferences and messaging. It was part of the organisation's identity. At times, this led to criticism. The College was seen by some as *too relational*, too soft. But that stance was intentional. Those who worked with the College understood that leadership was not just about competence, but about values, relationships and humanity.

Looking back, Steve is careful not to romanticise the past. He acknowledges that today's leaders are operating in an even more complex and pressured environment. Yet he expresses concern that some contemporary improvement approaches have become overly technical, more solution-driven than relationship-driven, more top-down than collaborative. In losing sight of relationships, he suggests, we risk losing the very conditions that make improvement sustainable.

When I asked what the profession loses when leaders feel unable to lead authentically, his response was both compassionate and practical. Leaders cannot change everything: poverty, policy, inspection frameworks. But they *can* focus on what is within their control: their teams, their culture, their daily interactions. Authentic leadership, he argues, is about resisting powerlessness: refusing to become a victim of the system or a lone hero trying to fix everything.

Instead, leaders must work *with* others, celebrate small wins and cultivate hope rather than despair. 'The only way people will follow you', Steve reflects, is 'if you're authentic'. In fragile systems, authenticity becomes not a luxury, but a stabilising force, the means by which trust is built, agency is sustained and communities endure.

'Why now' is also necessary because in the absence of strong, positive national and international leaders, it feels right to offer strategies and hope to those aspiring leaders and those already in the job. Leadership can, as I have said before, become all-consuming as we juggle competing priorities, shifting deadlines, challenging behaviours and parental complaints. In that context, to be able to pick up an easily digestible leadership book that reminds you "you're doing a great job" is a gift I willingly share.

Leading through crisis without losing humanity

The pandemic did not create all of education's challenges, but it exposed many of them. Schools closed, but leadership did not. Teachers taught through screens. Leaders juggled safeguarding, logistics, wellbeing and morale, often simultaneously. For a brief moment, the profession was publicly applauded. Then the applause faded, and the pressures remained.

Attendance declined. Behaviour became more complex, and for many leaders, these challenges did not disappear when classrooms reopened; they became embedded.

In this context, psychological safety is no longer a 'nice to have'. It is essential, not only for students, but for staff and leaders themselves. Where fear dominates, people retreat. Where trust is present, people stay, contribute and grow (Edmondson, 2018).

This is why authentic leadership matters now – not because leaders have all the answers but because honesty, humility and steadiness have become stabilising forces in uncertain systems.

If you are considering joining the profession now, join because this work matters more than ever and because it demands more than technical competence; it demands heart. To lead in schools today is to hold both high expectations and deep compassion. Authentic leadership, the kind that says 'I don't have all the answers, but I will listen, learn and act with integrity', models for young people how to live with courage in uncertain times. Lead with grace: be firm where necessary, but generous with patience; be principled but ready to apologise and change course when you're wrong. Those qualities create trusting cultures where teachers stay, pupils flourish and schools become resilient rather than brittle.

Part of the answer to *why now* is pragmatic: the system needs leaders who will stay. Recruitment targets continue to be missed, turnover remains visible and the cost of instability is felt daily in schools. But this moment is also an invitation.

For those considering entering the profession or stepping into leadership, this work matters more than ever. Not because it is easy, but because it demands more than technical competence. It demands character.

Authentic leaders retain teams not by promising perfection, but by modelling clarity, care and credibility. They reduce stress not by denying pressure, but by naming it honestly and acting with integrity. In doing so, they create cultures where people feel safe enough to commit and to stay.

What the evidence tells us about leadership and retention

When we interrogate the evidence, it illustrates the reason why, in this moment, this moment really does matter.

The urgency of authentic leadership is not only philosophical; it is evidenced. National workforce data paints a clear picture: the system can recruit teachers, but it struggles to retain them. Attrition accelerates over time, particularly in secondary schools and in subjects already under strain.

Research from the NFER and Education Support (NFER, 2023; Education Support, 2022, 2023) consistently shows that while workload and pay matter, retention is strongest where staff feel trusted, supported and professionally valued. In other words, people stay where leadership feels humane and purposeful and leave where it feels transactional or opaque.

The labour market, in this sense, becomes a mirror held up to leadership culture. Data does not just describe shortages; it reveals where belonging is present and where it is not.

Together, these reports form a compelling case for why now is the time to lead with both head and heart. The profession does not need louder slogans or new frameworks; it needs leaders who will model integrity, empathy and grace in the everyday act of showing up for others. That is how we rebuild trust, renew purpose and, ultimately, reimagine what it means to belong in education.

When we step back from individual experiences and look at the wider evidence, a consistent picture emerges. The education system is not struggling to attract people into teaching, but it is struggling to keep them. National data shows that fewer than six in ten teachers remain in the profession ten years after qualifying, with attrition particularly acute in the early years of a career. This pattern is not new, but it has accelerated in recent years and is now affecting leadership pipelines as well as classroom roles.

Independent analysis describes the workforce as being in a critical state, with vacancy rates rising and turnover becoming increasingly normalised. The impact is felt most sharply in secondary schools and trusts, where recruitment challenges are compounded by workload, accountability pressure and a shrinking pool of experienced leaders willing to step into senior roles. What is striking in much of this research is that pay and workload, while important, are rarely the sole reasons people leave.

Studies focusing on wellbeing and retention consistently highlight the role of leadership culture. Staff are more likely to stay in environments where they feel trusted, supported and able to raise concerns without fear. Where psychological safety is weak, stress increases, disengagement follows and departure becomes a rational act of self-preservation rather than a lack of resilience or commitment. In this context, leadership behaviour becomes a determining factor in whether people remain or walk away.

Taken together, the evidence reinforces what many leaders already sense. This moment is not simply about managing shortages or absorbing pressure. It is about the conditions leaders create and the signals they send about value, care and belonging. The data does not call for leaders to work harder or become tougher; it points instead to the urgent need for leadership that is intentional, relational and humane.

Leading the next generation

The teachers entering the profession today are not the same as those who joined even a decade ago. Many belong to Generation Z, digital natives shaped by the pandemic, global uncertainty and a growing insistence on purpose-driven work. They are ambitious but values-led, expecting not just fair pay, but flexibility, inclusion and meaningful autonomy. This generation has grown up seeing that work can happen anywhere, that wellbeing is not indulgent but essential and that hierarchy alone no longer guarantees respect. For school leaders, this means recruitment and retention can't rely on slogans about vocation or sacrifice. Instead, leadership must adapt to design workplaces that are relational, responsive and genuinely human.

Leadership reflection: Why now?

Take a moment to pause and look inward

It is easy, in education leadership, to become consumed by the noise: targets, timetables, tensions and to-do lists. Over time, that noise can distance leaders from the deeper questions, not just what needs doing, but what kind of culture is being created through the doing. This reflection is not about adding another task. It is about reconnecting with purpose in the midst of pressure.

The context described in this chapter may feel bigger than any one leader can change. But authentic leadership does not begin with control over the system; it begins with choices about how you show up within it. What you notice. What you tolerate. What you protect. What you are willing to name. The smallest leadership behaviours – the pause before responding, the honest 'I don't know yet', the clarity offered when others feel uncertain – can shape whether people feel safe enough to stay, speak and grow.

As you reflect, resist the urge to turn these questions into performance measures. Instead, treat them as a mirror. In a world that feels uncertain, your steadiness, compassion and consistency are not optional extras; they are part of the leadership strategy.

Reflect on leadership in context

- What does authentic leadership look like for you right now, in the context you serve?
- How have recent pressures shaped the way you lead consciously or unconsciously?
- Where might you need to pause and reconnect with what matters most?

Leadership is always shaped by the moment we are in.

Reflect on people, not just pressure

- As leaders, it is easy to become consumed by targets, timetables, tensions and to-do lists. How might this be showing up in your leadership?
- Behind the data on strain and attrition are individuals who once arrived hopeful and full of potential. How does your leadership help to protect that sense of hope?
- What signals does your culture send about whether people are expected to endure or supported to thrive?

Culture is experienced before it is measured.

Reflect on the next generation

- Think about the new generation of teachers entering your school. What are their expectations around trust, flexibility and voice?
- What might you do differently to help them see teaching not just as a job, but as a sustainable and purpose-filled career?
- How visible is your commitment to their development and wellbeing?

The future of the profession is shaped by today's leadership choices.

Reflect on everyday leadership

- Where do small moments offer opportunities for authenticity, the pause before responding, the honest 'I don't know', the quiet word of encouragement?
- How does your steadiness show up when others feel uncertain?
- In what ways do compassion and creativity feature in your leadership practice?

Authentic leadership is built in the ordinary moments.

Look ahead

- Before you turn the page, ask yourself: what will I do tomorrow that helps someone in my school feel seen, valued and safe enough to stay?

References

Edmondson, A. (2018). *The fearless organization: Creating psychological safety in the workplace for learning, innovation, and growth*. Wiley.

Education Support. (2023). *Teacher Wellbeing Index 2023*. Education Support.

National Foundation for Educational Research (NFER). (2023). *Teacher Labour Market in England Annual Report 2023*. NFER.

3 Vision and values

The DNA of authentic leadership

When vision and values are tested

Vision is easy to talk about when everything is calm. It appears neatly framed on walls, woven into school websites and rehearsed in presentations. Values, too, are often proudly displayed, articulated in statements that sound reassuringly familiar. But vision and values only become meaningful when they are tested when pressure rises, when the decision in front of you is uncomfortable, unpopular or personally costly.

Authentic leadership is revealed in those moments. Not in what leaders say they believe, but in what they choose to protect, challenge or walk away from when it would be easier to stay silent. Vision, at its core, is not about aspiration; it is about direction. Values are not decoration; they are the standards leaders fall back on when certainty disappears.

Research on values-led and ethical leadership consistently shows that vision and values become most influential during periods of uncertainty and pressure. Studies suggest that when leaders are required to make decisions with incomplete information or competing demands, clear values provide a cognitive and moral framework that supports judgement and reduces reactivity. Rather than limiting leadership action, values function as decision-making anchors, helping leaders prioritise what matters most when time, emotion and scrutiny are heightened. Evidence also indicates that leaders who consistently reference values when explaining decisions are perceived as more credible and trustworthy, even when outcomes are contested. In this way, vision and values are not abstract ideals but practical tools that shape behaviour, guide choices and sustain leadership integrity under pressure (Brown & Trevino, 2006; Heifetz et al., 2009).

Building shared vision and values

When I was appointed headteacher at Copthall in 2016, working with staff, students, governors and families on what our vision and values were going to be was the first thing I did. Having worked in schools where staff buy-in was not always

DOI: 10.4324/9781003635666-3

where it needed to be, and from my own personal experience as a child growing up in a school that had no clear direction and certainly no shared values, I knew getting this right was crucial.

And it worked.

Not because we found the perfect words, but because we treated vision and values as something to be *built together*, not imposed. From the outset, I was clear that this was not going to be an exercise in compliance or cosmetic change. I had no interest in producing a set of statements that would sit untouched on a website or be recited once a year in an inset session. I wanted our vision and values to become a shared language, something people could recognise themselves in and hold one another to account against.

We spent time listening. Not just to those who were already confident or invested, but to those who had felt unheard, disengaged or sceptical. Staff spoke honestly about what had been missing before: clarity, consistency and trust. Students talked about how school made them feel when they felt proud, and when they felt invisible. Families shared their hopes, but also their frustrations. Some of those conversations were uncomfortable. They surfaced tensions and past disappointments. But they mattered, because they told the truth.

What became clear very quickly was that people did not want lofty language or abstract ideals. They wanted to know what we stood for *in practice*. How would we treat one another when things went wrong? What would we prioritise when time, money and energy were stretched? What would not be tolerated, no matter how difficult it was to address?

Those questions shaped everything that followed.

Our values were deliberately simple, but not vague. They were chosen because they could be lived daily, tested publicly and referenced when decisions were challenged. Importantly, they were not neutral. They required action. They demanded courage. And they gave people permission and responsibility to name when our behaviour drifted away from what we said we believed.

Embedding those values was not a one-off moment. It was an ongoing discipline. They showed up in how we spoke to students, how we supported staff, how we handled mistakes and how we made decisions under pressure. When faced with necessary conversations, our values gave us a way in. When decisions were unpopular, they gave us a way to explain *why*. And when things went wrong as they inevitably did, they gave us a framework for repair.

What I learned in that first year of headship at Copthall is something I have carried with me ever since: vision and values do not create certainty, but they do create alignment. They do not remove the challenge, but they help people understand the *purpose* behind it. And perhaps most importantly, they make leadership feel less lonely. When values are truly shared, responsibility is no longer carried by one person at the top but held collectively.

That is when vision stops being an aspiration and becomes a compass, one that also protects leaders from mission creep.

Stated values vs lived values

Most schools can tell you what their values are. Far fewer can show you where they live.

In almost every school I have worked with, the values displayed on walls or websites are broadly similar: respect, ambition, integrity, kindness and community. There is nothing inherently wrong with these words. At Copthall, "respect" was chosen because it was easily understood and easily demonstrated. However, when student behaviour slipped and interactions became disrespectful, rather than launching into lengthy monologues about behaviour policy, we simply reminded students of the value they had chosen themselves. It grounded the conversation quickly and effectively. Shared values matter because they provide a common language when difficult conversations need to happen.

As part of our regular learning walks, we noticed a teacher who was not following the Department's schemes of work and was not pitching the lessons to meet the needs of every student. Aspiration was a value chosen by staff and students, and it was clear that this teacher was not being aspirational for the students nor himself. It was easy to challenge using our coaching model of feedback, grounded in our values. The teacher accepted his performance was not good enough, asked for help and agreed to follow the action points we had set out for him. I always used to say, it is difficult to argue with a system, process or expectations that people have co-created.

Research into organisational culture consistently highlights the distinction between espoused values and enacted values. Studies suggest that while leaders often articulate values clearly, it is everyday behaviour, decision-making and response to pressure that determine whether those values are believed. When there is misalignment between what leaders say and what they do, trust erodes quickly, even if intentions are positive. Conversely, consistency between stated values and lived experience strengthens credibility and provides staff with a reliable framework for interpreting leadership behaviour. Evidence also indicates that people are particularly attentive to how values are upheld in moments of difficulty, conflict or constraint. It is in these moments that values shift from aspiration to proof, shaping whether leadership feels authentic or performative (Schein, 2010).

The problem is not what is written down; it is what happens when those words are tested. Because values are not revealed in calm moments, they are revealed in conflict, in crisis and in the everyday decisions leaders make when no one is applauding.

Stated values are aspirational. Lived values are operational.

You see lived values in how leaders respond when standards slip, when behaviour challenges escalate or when someone is treated unfairly. You see them in whose voices are amplified and whose are quietly ignored. You see them in what is challenged immediately and what is allowed to drift. Over time, these patterns tell a far more honest story about what a school truly values than any carefully worded statement ever could.

This is where leadership becomes uncomfortable. Because lived values demand consistency, and consistency is hard when pressure is high. It is much easier to uphold values when decisions are popular, when resources are plentiful and when relationships are uncomplicated. It is far harder when a values-led decision risks conflict, criticism or personal cost.

I have seen schools proudly declare values around inclusion, fairness or high expectations, while simultaneously tolerating behaviours that undermine them. Leaders may justify this in the name of pragmatism, harmony or survival. But every time a value is compromised for convenience, it sends a message. Staff and students notice. They learn quickly which values are negotiable and which are not.

When values are compromised, it affects the reputation of a school. People notice the disconnect. They may hear leaders talk about aspiration as a core value, but then ask, "Aspiration for whom?" For me, aspiration should apply to every stakeholder. We should be aspirational for our parents, wanting the very best for their children; aspirational for our staff, supporting them to shape careers that work for them; aspirational for governors, ensuring they offer the right balance of support and challenge; and aspirational for ourselves as leaders, continuing to grow and learn from others.

Authentic leadership requires leaders to close the gap between what is stated and what is lived. That does not mean perfection. Values will always be tested, and leaders will sometimes get it wrong. What matters is the willingness to notice drift, to name it and to realign.

When leaders consistently return to their values, especially after missteps, trust grows. People understand that values are not slogans to be defended, but standards to be practised. Over time, this consistency creates cultural clarity. People know what to expect, what will be protected and what will be challenged.

This is the difference between values as decoration and values as discipline. And it is where authentic leadership is sustained

Inherited values vs chosen values

Not all values are chosen. Many are inherited, quietly absorbed from the culture's leaders, step into and rarely questioned in the early days of a role. They come embedded in systems, traditions, routines and expectations, shaping decision-making long before a leader has had the opportunity to reflect on whether they truly align with their own beliefs.

For new leaders, particularly those taking on headship for the first time, this inheritance can feel both comforting and constraining. There is reassurance in continuity, in respecting what has come before, and in not wanting to unsettle already fragile relationships. But there is also risk. When inherited values go unexamined, they can quietly dictate what is tolerated, what is avoided and whose voices carry weight.

Over time, leaders may find themselves enforcing norms that do not sit comfortably with them. Practices continue because '*this is how things have always been done*', not because they reflect a moral or educational conviction. The danger here is subtle but significant: leaders begin to compromise not through dramatic acts, but through small, repeated silences.

Choosing values requires a different kind of courage. It asks leaders to pause and ask difficult questions: *What do I stand for? What am I prepared to challenge? What am I willing to protect, even when it is uncomfortable?* This process is rarely neat. It can surface tension with colleagues, governing bodies or wider systems. But it is also where authentic leadership begins.

Because values that are consciously chosen, rather than passively inherited, become anchors. They give leaders a reference point when pressure mounts and clarity feels elusive. Without them, leadership drifts. With them, leaders may still face difficulty, but they do so with integrity.

My experience of the tensions this can bring came when I was a senior deputy in a large secondary school. An incoming Trust was focused, rightly, on raising standards. Leaders should never become complacent. However, standards in the school were already strong, staff were doing a good job, and yet there was an expectation that more needed to be done and done quickly.

One of the Trust's stated values was *ambition*, something few would argue against. For me, the tension lay not in the value itself, but in how that ambition was pursued.

This was an inherited value. I shared the ambition, but I was increasingly at odds with the methods being used to drive it. I believed and still believe that empathy, understanding, compassion and support elicit ambition in ways that directive or authoritarian leadership does not.

I chose to uphold the value of ambition by being authentically me. I focused on winning hearts and minds, working *with* staff rather than *to* them. Even when we reached exam season and the pressure intensified around securing the best possible outcomes, I remained anchored in my own values of compassion and respect. I wanted staff and students to perform at their best without feeling diminished or disposable in the process.

What I learned from this experience was that it is possible and necessary to adhere to a school's vision and values while enacting them in a way that aligns with your own moral compass. Authentic leadership does not require undermining shared goals or challenging values outright. It requires leaders to live those values with integrity, humanity and consistency.

This was a moment where inherited values became consciously chosen, not redefined, but reclaimed in a way that allowed me to lead with authenticity at my core.

Values as protection, not constraint

Values are often misunderstood as constraints, lines that limit what leaders can do or ideals that make leadership harder rather than easier. In reality, the opposite is true. When values are consciously chosen and consistently lived, they become one of the strongest forms of protection a leader has.

Leadership is relentless in its demand for decisions. Some are small and routine; others carry weight, consequence and scrutiny. Without clear values, leaders are left relying on instinct, emotion or the loudest voice in the room. Over time, this creates exhaustion. Decision fatigue sets in. Confidence wavers. Leadership begins to feel reactive rather than intentional.

Values interrupt that cycle.

When leaders are clear about what they stand for, decisions become anchored rather than ad hoc. Values provide a reference point when pressure mounts and opinions multiply. Values do not remove difficulty from leadership. But they do remove drift. And in uncertain times, that clarity is a form of protection.

Leadership rarely unravels in dramatic moments. It erodes slowly through competing demands, constant scrutiny and the pressure to keep everyone satisfied. School leaders, and particularly headteachers, often feel under the microscope: complaints, inspections, performance data, safeguarding and accountability. There is an unspoken fear that one mistake could become career-defining. This is precisely why clear values matter. When pressure builds, it becomes tempting to default to saying yes. People-pleasing can feel like the quickest route to keeping things moving. But the danger is subtle: how many times can a leader do that before their core values begin to erode? High-stakes accountability can lead to reactive decision-making, over-explaining and emotional exhaustion. I know this because I have been there.

Research into decision-making and leadership sustainability suggests that value clarity plays a protective role for leaders operating under sustained pressure. When leaders have a clear sense of their values, they are less likely to experience decision fatigue, moral distress or reactive behaviour in complex situations. Values function as an internal compass, reducing the cognitive load associated with constant judgement calls and helping leaders act with greater confidence and consistency. Evidence also indicates that values-led decision-making supports wellbeing by limiting the internal conflict that arises when leaders feel pulled in multiple directions. In this way, values do not constrain leadership; they protect it, enabling leaders to remain grounded, ethical and purposeful over time, even when circumstances are demanding or outcomes uncertain (West, 2021; Education Support, 2022).

I once worked with a colleague whose leadership style was experienced by many as abrupt and damaging, particularly by those she line-managed. Staff asked me to intervene, which I did. At the time, the school was under pressure to improve, and I was keen to maintain harmony within a newly formed leadership team. When she responded that she was simply being firm but fair, I accepted that explanation. In doing so, I prioritised keeping one relationship intact over staying true to my own value of compassion.

The result was that others felt unheard and unsupported. In trying to please one person, I had failed several others. With hindsight, it was clear that my values had been compromised not through malice but through avoidance. When complaints and distress continued, I knew I had to act differently. Challenging that behaviour was uncomfortable and emotionally demanding, but it was necessary. Staying silent would have been easier. It would not have been right.

Many things keep leaders awake at night, examinations, safeguarding and accountability, but knowing you have not acted in line with your values is often the one that lingers longest. Values act as a north star. They keep leaders grounded and authentic, even when doing so is difficult, even when it does not suit everyone.

That is their protective power.

When values pull in different directions

Values rarely exist in neat isolation. Leadership becomes most challenging not when values are absent, but when two values we hold both matter deeply and yet pull us in different directions: Compassion and ambition; Loyalty and integrity; Belonging and accountability. These tensions are not signs of weak leadership; they are evidence that leadership is real.

In moments like these, there is no perfect answer waiting to be discovered. Values-led leadership is not about finding the option that satisfies everyone, but about making decisions that align with what you stand for, even when that alignment comes at a cost. The discomfort leaders feel in these moments is not a sign that they are getting it wrong; it is often a sign that they are taking their responsibility seriously.

What makes these tensions particularly difficult is that both values involved often feel morally legitimate. Ambition matters. So does compassion. High expectations drive improvement. So does care for the people who are doing the work. When values collide, leaders can feel trapped between competing goods, each with its own consequences. The temptation in these moments is to delay, dilute or deflect, to search for a compromise that avoids discomfort altogether.

But values cannot always be blended without losing their integrity.

What I have learned is that clarity matters more than comfort. Leaders who attempt to hold every value at full strength, at all times, often end up paralysed or inconsistent. Instead, values led leadership requires prioritisation. It asks leaders to decide which value must take precedence *in this moment*, and to be transparent about why, but let's be clear, it does not mean abandoning other values.

When leaders act with clarity, they become visible. When they name their values, they make themselves accountable to them. This can feel risky, particularly in systems that reward compliance or quick fixes over considered judgement.

This is not comfortable leadership. But it is sustainable leadership. And in the long run, it is the kind that builds trust, even when decisions are contested.

Holding the line: Vision, values and authentic leadership

Vision and values are not static statements to be agreed once and left untouched. They are lived daily through the decisions leaders make, the behaviours they challenge and the compromises they refuse to accept. Over time, it is these small, often unremarkable moments that reveal what a leader truly stands for.

What becomes clear throughout this chapter is that vision provides direction, but values provide steadiness. They help leaders navigate complexity without losing themselves in the process. They offer protection when leadership feels lonely and clarity when external voices grow loud. And while values-led decisions do not always shield leaders from criticism, they do offer something more enduring: integrity.

There will be moments when values pull in different directions, when every option carries consequence, and when the path forward feels unclear. In those moments, authentic leadership is less about certainty and more about courage, the courage to act with intention, to explain decisions honestly and to remain grounded in what matters most.

Values do not make leadership easy. But they make it *possible* to lead well over time.

Vision and values, when lived with integrity, become more than guidance. They become a moral compass, one that allows leaders to move forward with confidence, even when the terrain is uncertain.

Leadership reflection

Values are often most visible when leaders speak about them in strategy documents, assemblies or moments of aspiration. But values are lived most clearly in quieter, less performative moments: how decisions are prioritised under pressure, how compromise is justified and how leaders respond when values collide rather than align. This reflection invites you to move beyond what you *say* you value and consider how those values are enacted in practice.

Leadership rarely offers choices between good and bad. More often, leaders navigate tensions between competing values: compassion and consistency, pace and care, loyalty and challenge. In these moments, values do not disappear; they are revealed. Authentic leadership is less about holding the 'right' values and more about recognising which values are shaping your decisions consciously or unconsciously when it would be easier to react than reflect.

The questions that follow are designed to help you notice patterns rather than isolated incidents. Over time, repeated small decisions communicate far more about values than singular statements ever could. People learn what matters in a system by observing what is protected, what is tolerated and what is quietly deprioritised. This is particularly true when leaders are under strain, fatigued or navigating competing demands.

As you reflect, allow yourself to sit with complexity. Values are not static or simple, and alignment is not a one-time achievement. It requires ongoing attention, self-awareness and the willingness to pause when decisions feel rushed or misaligned. Returning to values is not a sign of uncertainty; it is a discipline that sustains clarity, trust and integrity over time.

Take a moment to pause

Values often feel stable until they are tested. This reflection is an opportunity to look honestly at the values that guide your leadership, not as abstract statements, but as principles that shape everyday decisions, particularly under pressure.

Reflect on your core values

- Which values most strongly guide your leadership right now?
- Are these values consciously chosen, or quietly inherited from previous roles, cultures or leaders?
- How often do you name your values explicitly when making decisions?

Values are most powerful when they are intentional rather than assumed.

Reflect on values under pressure

- When demands conflict, which values tend to take precedence in your decisions?
- Where might you be compromising your values in the name of comfort, harmony or speed?
- How do you notice when pressure is beginning to distort your judgement?

Pressure reveals which values are truly non-negotiable.

Reflect on alignment and visibility

- How clearly could those around you articulate the values that guide your leadership?
- Where is there strong alignment between what you say you value and what others see you do?
- Where might there be small gaps between intention and impact?

Values become real through consistency, not intention alone.

Look ahead

- What is one decision you are currently facing where your values could offer greater clarity?
- What would it look like to lead that decision with intention rather than reaction?
- How will you make your values more visible in your leadership practice going forward?

References

Brown, M.E., Trevino, L.K. (2006). Ethical Leadership: A review and future directions. *The Leadership Quarterly, 17*(6), 595–616.

Education Support. (2022). *Teacher Wellbeing Index 2022.* Education Support.

Heifetz, R., Grashow, A., & Linsky, M (2009). *The Practice of Adaptive Leadership.* Harvard Business Press.

Schein, E. (2010). *Organizational Culture and Leadership.* Jossey-Bass.

West, M. (2021). *Compassionate Leadership.* Swirling Leaf Press.

4 Belonging

Belonging has become one of the most frequently used words in education, and, for some, one of the most misunderstood. It appears in strategy documents, trust values, recruitment brochures and inspection conversations, often positioned as something schools should *have* or *do*. Yet belonging is not an initiative, a programme or a slogan. It is a human experience. And in schools, it is foundational.

In 2024, the then Education Secretary spoke at the Confederation of School Trusts conference and articulated a concern that many school leaders recognised immediately:

> I want all children to achieve and thrive… A happy, healthy child who knows that deep down inside, they belong.
>
> The most recent data shows 1 in 3 fifteen-year-olds don't feel they belong in school… We've gone backwards, and we've fallen behind, and we've got to put this right.
>
> If we want to tackle the epidemic of school absence… children need to feel that they belong.

Few in the room would have disagreed. Belonging is not a radical idea; it is a basic human need. What *is* different now is the urgency with which it is being named. Attendance, behaviour, staff retention, wellbeing and engagement all point to the same truth: when people do not feel they belong, they disengage. Sometimes quietly. Sometimes visibly. Always with consequences.

Research consistently reinforces the relationship between belonging, engagement and sustained participation in school communities. Studies exploring attendance and pupil wellbeing highlight that students who feel connected to their school are more likely to attend regularly, engage in learning and seek support when they struggle (OECD – Student engagement & belonging 2021). Similarly, workforce research indicates that staff who experience a sense of belonging are more likely to remain in post, contribute beyond their formal role, and invest emotionally in the life of the school (Education Support, 2022; NFER, 2023). Belonging, in this sense,

DOI: 10.4324/9781003635666-4

is not an abstract ideal but a protective factor. It shapes how people experience challenge, respond to difficulty, and decide whether to stay or withdraw. When belonging is weak, absence and disengagement follow.

For those of us who have spent our lives working in schools, this should not come as a surprise. Teaching is a vocation. Most people enter the profession because they want to make a difference in the lives of young people. In doing so, they instinctively want those young people to feel safe, valued and included. The desire for belonging has always been there. What has not always been there is the intentionality to examine whether our systems, habits and leadership behaviours actually make belonging possible.

Belonging does not happen by accident. And it is not created by good intentions alone; when belonging is absent, its impact is rarely abstract.

Not being missed

When I speak to leaders, I often return to a story from my own schooling. I talk about riding the number 8 bus up and down Oxford Street on days when I should have been in class. I talk about truancy not as rebellion, but as disappearance. And I talk about the empty chair in the classroom, the one that represented me.

No one asked where I was.

No one followed up.

No one said, 'We missed you'.

Years later, I understand that what I experienced was not simply poor attendance tracking. It was the absence of belonging. I could be missing, and nothing shifted. My absence did not register. And when a child learns that they are not missed, they internalise something far more damaging than any sanction could convey.

Belonging is not about being present in a building. It is about being *noticed*. It is about knowing that your presence and your absence matter.

I often ask leaders to imagine the difference between two responses when a student returns after an unexplained absence. One is procedural: 'You need to catch up on the work you missed'. The other is relational: 'Welcome back. We missed you'. Both communicate expectations. Only one communicates belonging.

That difference is leadership, and it is in these small moments that belonging is either strengthened or lost.

From belonging to mattering

It was only later in my career, and most recently, when I encountered the work of Mohammed Abdallah, that language finally caught up with experience. Abdallah does not talk about belonging in isolation. Instead, he situates it within a wider framework of *mattering* and *becoming* (Abdallah, 2020).

He reminds us:

> The benefits of students feeling a strong sense of mattering, belonging and becoming are well-evidenced. The damage done by their absence is clear, too. These aren't abstract concepts; they show up in data, behaviour trends and engagement.

Abdallah's Mattering Model places mattering as the umbrella concept. People matter when they both *feel valued* (belonging) and are *given opportunities to add value* (becoming). These are not separate processes. They are mutually reinforcing.

Belonging enables becoming.

When people feel safe, accepted and seen, they are more likely to take risks, contribute and step forward. A student who feels they belong is far more willing to engage, to try and to persist.

Becoming reinforces belonging.

When people are trusted with responsibility, voice and agency, they do not simply feel included; they feel essential. They move from being participants to contributors.

Research exploring the concept of mattering reinforces the idea that belonging alone is not enough to sustain engagement or wellbeing (OECD, 2021; West, 2021). Studies in organisational and educational psychology suggest that people are more likely to thrive when they believe they are noticed, valued and able to contribute meaningfully, not simply included. Mattering is closely linked to voice, agency and recognition; it shapes whether individuals feel their presence makes a difference to outcomes, decisions and culture. In school settings, this distinction is significant. Staff and pupils may technically belong to an institution, yet still feel invisible or replaceable. Evidence suggests that when leaders actively signal that individuals matter through listening, explanation and opportunities for influence, trust deepens and commitment strengthens. Mattering, therefore, transforms belonging from a passive state into an active relationship between leaders and those they serve.

This reinforcing loop sits at the heart of mattering. The more people feel they belong, the more they contribute. The more they contribute, the deeper their sense of significance becomes.

For leaders, this matters profoundly. Because it reframes belonging not as something passive, *something we give*, but as something dynamic that is shaped by culture, opportunity and trust.

Belonging is not niceness

One of the most persistent myths in education is that belonging is about being nice. It is not. Belonging is about clarity, consistency and care. It is about knowing where you stand. And it is about being held to standards that protect the collective.

This is where belonging connects directly to leadership behaviour.

In schools where belonging is strong, expectations are clear and fairly applied. People are challenged because they are valued. Conversations are had, not avoided. Accountability is not punitive, but purposeful. In these environments, people may not always feel comfortable, but they feel secure.

By contrast, schools that confuse belonging with comfort often drift. Inconsistencies grow. Silence replaces honesty. Issues are left unaddressed in the name of harmony. Over time, this erodes trust and fractures belonging, particularly for those who already feel marginalised.

Belonging depends on clarity. And clarity requires leadership courage.

Listening as a leadership act

While writing this chapter, I revisited Rachel Higginson's work on authentic listening. Her challenge to leaders is deceptively simple: *stop messing around and listen*. Not to respond. Not to judge. But to understand.

Higginson describes belonging as a slow peeling away of institutional consciousness, the unspoken habits, assumptions and inherited practices that shape how people experience school. She invites leaders to listen deeply enough to surface uncomfortable truths, because without truth, belonging cannot grow.

Listening, in this sense, is not passive. It is an active leadership stance.

It requires leaders to notice who speaks and who does not. Whose concerns are acted upon quickly, and whose are deferred. Whose discomfort is legitimised, and whose is minimised.

When communities are genuinely listened to, belonging begins to take root. Not because every issue is resolved immediately, but because people feel seen.

Higginson uses the idea of a *Fingerprint Culture* to describe environments that intentionally hear, see and flex so that individual beauty is reflected. This is not about lowering expectations or fragmenting standards. It is about recognising that uniformity is not the same as equity, and that belonging often requires systems to adapt, not people to disappear parts of themselves.

Walking the school in someone else's shoes

One of the simplest, yet most powerful, leadership exercises I use with senior teams is this: walk your school through the eyes of someone who does not sit at the centre of power. This exercise is not symbolic. It is diagnostic.

A student with Special Educational Needs and Disabilities.

A parent for whom English is not their first language.

A member of staff from a global majority background.

A new teacher navigating unspoken norms.

A child who is frequently sanctioned.

Ask yourself:

Where would they feel welcomed?

Where would they feel tolerated rather than included?

Where might they feel invisible?

This is not about blame. It is about awareness. You cannot create belonging until you are willing to see who is currently standing on the margins.

Belonging as leadership DNA

Belonging is not an add-on. It is leadership DNA.

The leaders who leave the deepest imprint are not always those with the loudest presence or the longest lists of initiatives. They are the ones who make people feel seen; who notice absence as much as attendance; who hold standards without stripping dignity.

Culture is not built into strategy documents. It is built into corridors, classrooms and conversations. It is built into how leaders respond when things go wrong. It is built into whether people feel safe to speak, to fail and to try again.

Belonging is revealed in policy, too: behaviour policies; attendance procedures; flexible working arrangements; and recruitment decisions. Each one sends a signal about who the system is designed for and who must adapt to survive within it.

Belonging is not soft.

It is structural.

It is systemic.

And it is shaped, every day, by leadership behaviour.

Staff belonging: The engine of school culture

It is impossible to talk honestly about belonging without talking about adults.

Schools often focus their belonging efforts on students, and rightly so. But when staff do not feel they belong, the culture begins to fracture in ways that children inevitably feel. Belonging is not something leaders can deliver to students while withholding it from adults. It does not work that way.

Staff belonging is created through everyday leadership behaviours: whether voices are genuinely heard, whether concerns are addressed rather than deflected, whether people feel psychologically safe to speak honestly without fear of reprisal. It shows up in how workload is discussed, how mistakes are handled and how decisions are communicated.

In schools where staff belong, you can feel it. There is a sense of collective responsibility rather than quiet compliance. People support one another. They challenge with care. They stay.

In schools where staff do not belong, the symptoms are different but just as telling. Conversations move to car parks and corridors. Innovation slows. Absence rises. People remain physically present but emotionally detached. They do what is required, but no more. This is not a failure of professionalism; it is a response to not feeling safe.

Research into school culture and workforce sustainability consistently highlights staff belonging as a critical factor in retention, wellbeing and organisational effectiveness. Studies examining teacher attrition suggest that decisions to leave are rarely driven by workload alone, but by the cumulative experience of feeling unsupported, unheard or disconnected from leadership. Evidence from workforce wellbeing research indicates that when staff feel psychologically safe, trusted and valued, they are more likely to remain engaged, contribute discretionary effort and invest in relationships with pupils and colleagues. Conversely, environments where belonging is weak often see higher levels of absence, reduced collaboration and a narrowing of professional risk-taking. Staff belonging, therefore, is not an optional cultural extra; it is a foundational condition for sustaining healthy school communities and protecting the people within them (Education Support, 2022; NFER, 2023).

Leaders sometimes underestimate the emotional labour staff carry simply by showing up. Teaching is relational work. It requires energy, empathy and resilience. When that labour is not acknowledged or protected, belonging erodes.

Creating staff belonging does not mean removing accountability or lowering expectations. In fact, the opposite is true. Adults feel safest in environments where expectations are clear, standards are fair and conversations are prioritized rather than avoided. Belonging thrives where clarity and care coexist.

Micro-behaviours: How culture is really communicated

Belonging is rarely created through grand gestures. It is shaped through micro-behaviours, the small, often unnoticed actions that accumulate into culture.

You can walk into a school and understand its culture within minutes by noticing:

Who leaders greet and who they overlook.

Whether names are pronounced correctly.

How staff speak to students when no one is watching.

Whether ideas are interrupted or explored.

How mistakes are responded to.

Who feels confident enough to speak in meetings.

These micro-behaviours are the grammar of belonging. Individually, they seem insignificant. Collectively, they communicate powerful messages about who matters and who does not.

A leader who consistently acknowledges staff effort builds trust without saying a word. A leader who only speaks when something goes wrong erodes belonging, even if unintentionally. A raised eyebrow, a sigh and a delayed response are all read for meaning.

Belonging lives in these moments. And because micro-behaviours are habitual, they require conscious leadership to change. Leaders must notice themselves as much as they notice others.

When belonging fails

The emotional cost of not belonging

We often talk about belonging as something positive, but its absence carries a significant emotional cost.

For students, not belonging can show up as withdrawal, disengagement, masking or behaviour that seeks attention at any cost. Children who do not feel they belong may decide early on that school is not for them. Once that narrative takes hold, it is hard to undo.

For staff, the cost is quieter but just as damaging. People stop contributing ideas. They stop volunteering. They stop challenging decisions they know are flawed. Over time, they shrink themselves to fit the space they believe is available.

This is not apathy. It is protection.

Schools cannot thrive when children are in survival mode, and adults are emotionally exhausted. Belonging is not an optional extra. It is the soil in which well-being, learning and growth are rooted.

Belonging, accountability and necessary conversations

Belonging is often misunderstood as the absence of challenge. In reality, it depends on it.

As explored in Chapter 8, on Necessary Conversations, avoiding accountability is not kind leadership. It is destabilising. People feel safest when they know where they stand. They feel valued when leaders care enough to speak honestly and act consistently.

Necessary conversations, when handled with dignity, are acts of belonging. They communicate: *you matter enough to be told the truth; this community matters enough to protect its standards; and growth is expected, not optional.*

When leaders avoid these conversations, belonging is quietly undermined. Silence creates uncertainty. Inconsistency breeds resentment. And those who already feel marginalised are often the first to disengage.

Belonging and accountability are not opposing forces. They are mutually reinforcing. One cannot exist sustainably without the other.

When silence breaks belonging

There is a moment in my career that fundamentally reshaped how I understand staff belonging not as an abstract idea, but as a line that, once crossed, cannot be repaired.

I was a deputy headteacher in a school facing significant challenges: low standards, limited resources and fragile staff morale. I was working relentlessly, pushing expectations, holding boundaries and trying to raise the bar in an environment where doing so was not always welcomed. It was difficult work, but I believed in it. I believed in the school.

During this time, I challenged a member of staff for repeatedly failing to sign in and out during breaks, a basic professional expectation. What followed was something I could not have anticipated. I was informed that this member of staff had been overheard referring to me using a highly racist and offensive term. I did not hear the comment directly, but it was reported to me by others.

When I raised this with the headteacher, his response was simple and devastating:

You weren't there, so there's nothing I can do.

In that moment, belonging fractured.

What hurt most was not only the comment itself, though that mattered deeply, but the silence that followed. The message was clear: my dignity was negotiable. My safety was conditional. The harm caused to me was secondary to the discomfort of acting.

Another colleague later challenged that decision, rightly questioning the leadership response. An investigation was eventually launched, and the member of staff was dismissed. But by then, the damage had already been done. I had handed in my notice. For me, this was a red line.

I could not remain in a place where racism was met first with inaction, where leadership hesitated to protect belonging until challenged and where the burden of that hesitation fell on the person who had been harmed.

This was not a dramatic exit. It was a values-based one.

Belonging is not destroyed only by overt hostility. It is destroyed just as effectively by silence. By leaders choosing not to act. By decisions that communicate, intentionally or not, *this is not serious enough to disrupt the status quo.*

The headteacher later apologised. I accepted that apology. But apologies do not undo the moment when trust breaks. Belonging, once lost in that way, is not easily restored.

This experience reinforced something I now hold as a leadership truth: *staff do not leave schools because expectations are high; they leave when their dignity is not protected.* They leave when leadership signals through action or inaction that some forms of harm can be tolerated.

Belonging requires courage. It requires leaders to act even when it is uncomfortable, inconvenient, or contested. Because when leaders do not act, the message to those affected is unmistakable: *you are on your own.*

And no one belongs in a place where silence speaks louder than values.

Belonging as a shared responsibility

Although leadership behaviour is critical, belonging cannot live solely in the headteacher's office. It is a shared responsibility, enacted through classrooms, meetings, playgrounds and policies.

Schools that embed belonging effectively tend to:

Name and challenge deficit language.

Create meaningful opportunities for student and staff voice.

Treat mistakes as learning rather than ammunition.

Design policies that protect dignity as well as standards.

Model repair when things go wrong.

Belonging is strengthened when people see leaders acknowledge missteps and take responsibility. Repair is powerful. It signals humility and humanity. It tells people that belonging does not require perfection, only honesty.

From belonging to becoming

Belonging is not the endpoint. It is the foundation.

When people feel they belong, they are more willing to become. They take risks. They step forward. They invest. They lead.

Students who belong are more likely to see themselves as capable learners and future contributors. When they see themselves represented in the curriculum in a positive way, students will become critical thinkers and may feel more encouraged to speak up rather than stay silent. Staff who belong are more likely to innovate, mentor others and stay committed to the profession.

This is where leadership has its greatest impact. Not in controlling outcomes, but in creating conditions where people can grow into themselves.

Together, belonging, becoming and mattering create a culture of commitment rather than compliance.

The courage to lead for belonging

Belonging is not an initiative to be launched or a statement to be displayed. It is an ongoing act of leadership courage. It requires leaders to examine their systems, confront uncomfortable truths and pay attention to the small, everyday behaviours that shape experience.

It asks leaders to notice who is missing, who is silent and who is carrying the weight. It asks them to listen deeply, act consistently and hold standards without stripping dignity.

When belonging is present, people take risks. They speak honestly. They grow.

When it is absent, they retreat, disengage or disappear.

Authentic leadership lives here, in the willingness to lead with humanity and clarity at the same time. When leaders get this right, schools become places where people can say with confidence:

I am seen.

I am valued.

I belong.

And from that place, everything else becomes possible.

Leadership reflection: Belonging in practice

Belonging is often spoken about with confidence, yet experienced unevenly. Leaders may genuinely believe they are creating inclusive, welcoming environments, while others quietly feel invisible, tolerated rather than valued or uncertain whether they truly matter. This reflection invites you to pause and examine belonging not as an intention, but as an experience shaped by leadership behaviour, systems and everyday interactions.

Belonging is revealed in small moments: whose voices are heard, how difference is responded to, how absence is interpreted and how people are treated when they struggle or disagree. It is reinforced through systems as much as relationships. Policies, routines and informal norms all communicate who is prioritised, who is protected and who is expected to adapt. Leaders do not create belonging through statements alone, but through the consistency with which dignity, curiosity and fairness are upheld.

The questions that follow are designed to help you look beneath the surface. They ask you to consider where belonging may be unintentionally undermined, particularly for those with less power, visibility or confidence to speak. This is not about blame or judgement; it is about awareness. Authentic leadership requires the courage to notice where good intentions do not always translate into equitable experiences.

Before looking outward, it can be helpful to turn the lens inward. Many leaders have their own experiences of feeling on the margins, moments when they were overlooked, underestimated, unheard or expected to adapt quietly in order to belong. These experiences may come from earlier in life, from previous roles, or from spaces where identity, power or difference shaped how welcome they felt.

Taking time to recall those moments is not about reopening old wounds, but about reconnecting with empathy. How did it feel to be on the edges rather than at the centre? What behaviours, systems or silences contributed to that experience? And what stayed with you long after the moment passed?

Leaders who are willing to reflect on their own experiences of belonging and exclusion are often better able to notice when others may be navigating similar feelings. This self-awareness does not guarantee perfect inclusion, but it strengthens compassion, sharpens curiosity and grounds leadership decisions in lived understanding rather than assumption.

As you reflect, pay attention to discomfort. Discomfort is often a signal that something important is being surfaced. Creating cultures of belonging requires leaders to stay present in that discomfort, to listen carefully, and to act thoughtfully even when the answers are not straightforward. Belonging is not a one-time achievement; it is a responsibility that must be returned to repeatedly, especially when pressure, fatigue, or habit make it easier to look away.

Take a moment to pause

Belonging is easy to speak about in principle, but far harder to examine honestly in practice. These reflections are not about judgement; they are about awareness.

Reflect on your leadership behaviour

- When was the last time someone challenged your decision? How did you respond? with curiosity, defensiveness or silence?
- Whose voices are most often heard in your school, and whose are easiest to overlook?
- How do you typically respond when an issue feels uncomfortable, complex or inconvenient?

Belonging is shaped not by what leaders say they value, but by how they behave when values are tested.

Reflect on systems and culture

- Where in your policies or routines might belonging unintentionally be undermined?
- Which groups of staff or students are most likely to feel marginalised by 'the way things are done here'?
- How do your systems respond to harm, particularly when it involves power, identity or prejudice?

Systems communicate belonging just as loudly as relationships.

Reflect on courage and accountability

- Are there moments when silence feels easier than action? What does that silence communicate to others?
- How confident are you that every member of your community would feel protected if they raised a concern?
- Where might avoiding necessary conversations be eroding trust or belonging, even unintentionally?

Belonging cannot coexist with avoidance.

Reflect on staff belonging

- Do your staff feel safe to be honest with you?
- How do you know?
- When mistakes are made, is the focus on learning or blame?

Adults who feel they belong are better able to create belonging for children.

Look ahead

- What one leadership behaviour could you change tomorrow that would strengthen belonging in your community?
- Where might acting with greater clarity rather than greater comfort better protect dignity?
- How will you ensure that belonging is not just spoken about, but actively upheld?

References

Abdallah, M. (2020). The Mattering Model: What if Belonging Is Only 50% of the Answer? Substack article.

Education Support. (2022). *Teacher Wellbeing Index 2022*. Education Support.

NFER. (2023). Teacher Labour Market in England Annual Report 2023.

OECD. (2021). *Student engagement and belonging.*

West, M. (2021). *Compassionate Leadership*. Swirling Leaf Press.

5 Mission, strategy and accountability (without losing yourself)

Why mission matters more than ever

In periods of relative calm, mission can feel like something leaders return to ceremonially rather than practically. It appears in vision statements, strategic plans and inspection documents, often expressed in carefully chosen language that signals intent. But in times of sustained pressure, mission either becomes a stabilising force or fades quietly into the background, replaced by urgency, compliance and reaction.

Mission as an anchor, not a slogan

In the current educational landscape, leaders are operating in conditions that rarely allow for pause. Competing priorities, heightened accountability, workforce instability and constant external scrutiny mean that decisions are often made at pace and under pressure. In this context, mission is no longer a luxury or an abstract ideal; it is the anchor that prevents drift.

When purpose blurs, work multiplies

When mission is unclear, strategy becomes fragmented. Leaders find themselves responding to the loudest demand rather than the most important one, prioritising what is urgent over what is meaningful. Over time, this reactive mode erodes coherence. Initiatives multiply, workload increases and people struggle to see how their efforts connect to a shared purpose. The work continues, but the why becomes blurred.

Mission drift and the quiet slide into reactivity

This is often where loss of strategic clarity begins. Not as a dramatic shift in direction, but as a gradual accumulation of small decisions made under pressure. When

DOI: 10.4324/9781003635666-5

times are hard, leaders can become so focused on responding, firefighting and holding things together that they stop 'sweating the small things' that once protected purpose. Initiatives are added rather than interrogated. Exceptions become routine. The connection between daily practice and core mission loosens.

This kind of strategic drift rarely feels like a choice. It feels like a necessity. Over time, however, it pulls leaders away from what they most want to protect.

Research into organisational leadership under sustained pressure highlights mission drift as a common risk when leaders are required to respond continuously to competing demands. Studies suggest that in high-accountability environments, leaders are more likely to prioritise immediacy and compliance over coherence, particularly when time and capacity are constrained (Fullan, 2014). This does not typically result from a loss of commitment to purpose, but from cumulative decision-making made under stress. Evidence indicates that without deliberate mechanisms to revisit mission, organisations can experience strategic overload, diluted focus and increased workload without corresponding impact. In this context, mission drift becomes less about poor leadership judgement and more about the absence of protected space to reflect, prioritise and say no. Recognising mission drift as a structural risk, rather than a personal failing, is an important step in sustaining purposeful leadership over time.

Mission matters because it provides a reference point when everything else feels unstable. It allows leaders to test decisions against a deeper purpose: *Does this align with what we are here to do?* When leaders are grounded in mission, they are better able to say no to distractions, to sequence change thoughtfully and to protect what matters most, even when external pressures push in other directions.

This does not mean that mission remains static. Effective leaders understand that mission must be lived and interpreted, not simply preserved. As contexts shift, leaders are required to return to mission repeatedly, asking how core values are enacted in new circumstances. This reflective return to purpose is what allows mission to remain relevant rather than rhetorical.

Mission as moral compass

In schools and trusts, mission also serves as a moral compass. It shapes how leaders balance competing demands, particularly when those demands pull in different ethical directions. Decisions about resource allocation, staffing, curriculum and support for vulnerable learners are rarely neutral. When mission is explicit and shared, it offers a principled framework for navigating these tensions with greater integrity.

Mission enables autonomy

Importantly, mission is not just for leaders. When articulated clearly and enacted consistently, it helps others make sense of their work. Staff are more likely to exercise professional judgement with confidence when they understand the purpose guiding decisions. Autonomy becomes possible because people know what they are working towards, not just what they are expected to do.

When accountability detaches from meaning

In the absence of mission-led leadership, accountability can become disconnected from meaning. Targets, measures and outcomes begin to stand in for purpose, rather than serve it. Leaders may find themselves meeting external expectations while feeling increasingly misaligned internally. This is often the point at which leadership begins to feel performative rather than authentic.

Re-centring mission is therefore not about retreating from accountability or ambition. It is about ensuring that strategy and action remain connected to the values that brought leaders into the work in the first place. Mission permits leaders to be intentional rather than reactive, to act with discernment rather than speed alone.

In a system that constantly demands more, mission provides the discipline to decide what matters most. It reminds leaders that not every pressure requires the same response, and that sustained impact comes from coherence rather than accumulation. Holding mission at the centre of leadership practice is not an act of nostalgia; it is a practical necessity for leading well without losing direction or self.

Strategy as values in action

Strategy is often spoken about as a technical exercise: plans, priorities, milestones and measures. In schools and trusts, it is frequently associated with improvement plans, frameworks and performance cycles. While these tools have their place, they can obscure a more fundamental truth: strategy is not neutral. Every strategic choice reflects what leaders value, whether consciously or not.

Strategy is not neutral

At its core, strategy is simply values made visible through decision-making.

Leaders reveal their values not through what they say, but through what they prioritise, resource and protect. When values and strategy are aligned, intention and action are coherent. When they are not, staff experience confusion, frustration and mistrust. Over time, this misalignment erodes credibility far more quickly than any single unpopular decision.

Culture and strategy: Not rivals but reinforcers

Leadership literature often contrasts culture and strategy, most famously through the assertion that *culture eats strategy for breakfast*. While this observation usefully highlights the power of lived behaviour over written plans, it can oversimplify the relationship between the two. In practice, culture and strategy are not competing forces. Culture reflects what is tolerated and rewarded; strategy reveals what is chosen and prioritised (Schein, 2010).

When strategy is disconnected from values, culture will always undermine it. But when strategy is deliberately shaped by values, it becomes one of the most powerful ways leaders influence culture over time. What leaders choose to invest in, protect and pursue sends a clearer message than any statement of intent. In this sense, strategy does not replace culture; it shapes it.

Overload as a symptom of weak strategy

One of the clearest indicators of weak strategy is overload. When leaders struggle to articulate what matters most, everything begins to matter equally. Initiatives accumulate, and priorities multiply, often without a clear sense of what matters. Staff are asked to do more, often without a clear sense of why. In these conditions, strategy becomes reactive rather than intentional, and values are diluted by volume.

The discipline of saying no

Strong strategy, by contrast, is defined as much by what leaders choose *not* to do as by what they pursue. This requires discipline and courage. Saying no to additional initiatives, to short-term fixes, to external demands that do not align with mission can feel risky, particularly in systems where leaders are judged by visible activity. Yet without this restraint, strategy becomes indistinguishable from busyness. This is why a values-led strategy requires restraint as much as ambition.

Make trade-offs, speakable

Values-led strategy also requires leaders to be explicit about trade-offs. Every strategic decision carries opportunity cost. Time, energy and attention invested in one area are unavailable elsewhere. When leaders are honest about these trade-offs, they build trust. When trade-offs remain unspoken, people are left to make sense of decisions on their own, often assuming inconsistency or favouritism where none was intended.

Strategy drifts through exhaustion

This is where over-extension of focus often takes hold. Under sustained pressure, leaders may feel compelled to respond to every demand, inspection focus or emerging priority. Small deviations accumulate. Temporary measures become permanent. Over time, strategy drifts away from mission, not through neglect, but through exhaustion. Values remain stated but are no longer enacted consistently.

Reclaiming strategy as values in action requires leaders to return repeatedly to purpose and ask difficult questions: *What problem are we actually trying to solve? Who does this decision serve? What does success look like in practice, not just on paper?* These questions slow decision-making, but they also sharpen it. They help leaders distinguish between activity and impact.

Importantly, a values-led strategy does not remove accountability. It reframes it. When strategy is clearly connected to mission, accountability becomes about progress towards shared purpose rather than compliance with disconnected measures. People are more likely to engage meaningfully with targets and expectations when they understand how these contribute to something larger than performance alone.

Strategy creates the conditions for agency

This approach also supports professional agency, autonomy and retention. When leaders are clear about strategic intent, they can afford to loosen control over how outcomes are achieved. Staff are better able to exercise judgement, innovate and adapt when they understand the boundaries within which they are working. Autonomy thrives not in the absence of strategy, but in its clarity.

Strategy, then, is not an abstract plan held at a senior level. It is a living expression of leadership values, enacted daily through decisions large and small. It is visible in where leaders spend their time, what they pay attention to and what they allow to continue unchallenged. When strategy is aligned with mission, it creates coherence, focus and trust even in complex and pressured contexts. Research consistently highlights the relationship between sustained pressue and attrition (Education Support, 2022; NFER, 2023).

Autonomy, trust and distributed leadership

Autonomy is built in a relationship with trust

Autonomy is often spoken about as something leaders grant. In practice, it is something that is built slowly, deliberately and in relationship with trust.

In schools and trusts, calls for autonomy frequently sit alongside increased accountability and oversight. Leaders are asked to empower others while simultaneously being held responsible for outcomes they do not fully control. This tension can make autonomy feel risky. Without clarity, it can quickly slide into anxiety for leaders and staff alike.

Autonomy without trust can feel exposing; trust without clarity quickly becomes destabilising.

Autonomy needs clarity

When leaders are clear about mission and strategy, autonomy becomes possible. People are better able to make decisions when they understand the purpose guiding them and the boundaries within which they are working. In these conditions, autonomy is not about doing whatever one chooses; it is about exercising professional judgement in service of shared goals.

Delegation vs distributed leadership

Distributed leadership is not the same as delegation. Delegation assigns tasks; distributed leadership shares responsibility. It asks leaders to let go of control over process while retaining accountability for purpose and outcomes. This shift is challenging, particularly for leaders who have progressed by being highly competent, responsive and reliable themselves. Letting go can feel like losing grip, rather than building capacity.

When control tightens, ownership shrinks

Where autonomy is absent, leaders often compensate by over-monitoring. Systems multiply. Checks increase. Approval is required for decisions that once sat comfortably at team level. While this may provide short-term reassurance, it rarely builds long-term confidence. Over time, it signals a lack of trust and erodes ownership. People become compliant rather than committed, waiting to be told rather than thinking critically.

High responsibility, low authority

This is reflected in a familiar frustration voiced by teachers and leaders alike: *why do I have to jump through so many hoops to get something fairly straightforward signed off?* We expect a great deal from our middle leaders; they are, in many ways, the engine room of our schools, yet too often we fall short of giving them the autonomy they need to grow. When responsibility is high, but authority is limited, leadership becomes performative rather than developmental.

Research into professional agency and leadership capacity in education consistently highlights autonomy as a key factor in motivation, development and retention. Studies suggest that when individuals are trusted to exercise judgement aligned to shared purpose, they are more likely to take ownership of outcomes and invest in long-term improvement. Conversely, environments characterised by high responsibility and low autonomy are associated with increased frustration, risk aversion and disengagement. Evidence also indicates that excessive monitoring and approval structures can unintentionally signal a lack of trust, undermining confidence and reducing leadership capacity over time. Autonomy, therefore, is not simply a cultural preference but a strategic condition that enables systems to grow leaders rather than contain them.

Autonomy without support can become isolation

Conversely, autonomy that is not supported by shared understanding can place unfair pressure on individuals. When expectations are unclear or when leaders step back without explanation, autonomy can feel isolating rather than empowering. This is particularly true for early career staff and those stepping into leadership for the first time. Support, guidance and permission to learn matter as much as freedom.

Trust makes autonomy feel safe

Trust sits at the centre of this balance. Leaders build trust by being consistent, by explaining decisions and by following through. When people trust that leadership intent is fair and values-driven, they are more willing to take responsibility, to act with initiative and to learn from mistakes. Trust makes autonomy feel safe.

Distributed leadership also requires leaders to tolerate differences. When autonomy is real, decisions will not always look the same across teams or settings. Approaches will vary. Pace will differ. Leaders must decide which differences matter and which reflect healthy professional judgement. This discernment is part of the discipline of leadership.

Importantly, autonomy does not remove accountability; it relocates it. Responsibility moves closer to practice, while leaders retain oversight of alignment and impact. When accountability conversations are framed around purpose rather than compliance, people are more likely to engage openly and take ownership of outcomes.

At scale: Autonomy without fragmentation

At scale, this work becomes even more complex. Leaders operating across multiple schools or teams cannot be everywhere at once. Autonomy and distributed leadership are not optional in these contexts; they are necessary. The challenge is ensuring that autonomy does not become fragmentation. Mission and strategy provide the connective tissue that holds distributed systems together.

Leaders who succeed in building autonomous, trust-rich cultures are often those who resist the pull to centralise when pressure increases. Instead, they invest time in building shared understanding, developing leadership capacity at all levels and creating structures that support thoughtful decision-making. This work is slower than issuing directives, but it is far more sustainable.

Ultimately, autonomy, trust and distributed leadership are expressions of belief, belief in people, in purpose and in the capacity of a system to learn. When leaders hold this belief alongside clarity and accountability, they create conditions where leadership is not concentrated at the top, but enacted throughout the organisation.

Determination, pace and staying the course

Determination is discernment, not force

Determination in leadership is often misunderstood. It is sometimes equated with stubbornness, relentless drive or the ability to push through at all costs. In reality, determination is less about force and more about discernment. It is the capacity to remain committed to purpose over time, particularly when progress is slow, resistance is present or external pressure intensifies.

Rhythm over rush

In complex educational settings, leaders are frequently required to operate at pace. Urgent issues demand attention. Competing priorities pull focus in multiple directions. In these conditions, the temptation is to move quickly, to demonstrate action and to seek visible momentum. While speed has its place, sustained leadership impact depends far more on rhythm than rush.

Staying the course requires leaders to distinguish between persistence and rigidity. Not every challenge signals the need for a change in direction. Equally, not every obstacle should be pushed through without reflection. Determined leaders learn to read context carefully, asking when to hold firm and when to adapt. This judgement is developed over time and is shaped by values, experience and self-awareness.

Pace shapes commitment

Pace matters because it shapes how change is experienced by others. When leaders move too quickly without securing understanding or commitment, even well-intentioned initiatives can falter. People may comply outwardly while disengaging internally. Conversely, moving too slowly can communicate uncertainty or a lack of conviction. Finding the right pace is not about perfect calibration; it is about attentiveness to people as well as outcomes.

When fatigue tests your purpose

Determination is also tested in moments of fatigue. Educational leadership is emotionally demanding, particularly when leaders are holding responsibility for others' wellbeing alongside performance expectations. Over time, the cumulative weight of decision-making, scrutiny and care can erode energy and clarity. Leaders may begin to question whether the effort required to sustain change is worth the personal cost.

Resilience is not a substitute for support

In these moments, resilience is often invoked as a badge of honour, *you will have to dig deep; this is just part of the job.* While resilience is undoubtedly needed, framing it as the primary solution can imply that endurance is the only acceptable response to unsustainable conditions. This risks individualising what are often systemic pressures. When resilience becomes synonymous with simply coping, rather than being supported to thrive, even the most committed leaders may begin to withdraw. This moment of doubt is one of the factors contributing to the loss of talented teachers, support staff, governors and leaders from the sector, a loss schools can ill afford.

This is often where values are most at risk. When leaders are tired, under pressure or isolated, it becomes harder to hold boundaries, revisit purpose and resist drift. Short-term relief can feel more appealing than long-term integrity. Staying the course in these moments is not about heroism; it is about returning, again and again, to the reasons the work matters.

Future leaders and the discipline of staying

Earlier in my leadership journey, my understanding of mission was shaped through my involvement in the Future Leaders programme. The premise was both simple and demanding: aspiring leaders would be placed in some of the most challenging schools, guided by a clear moral commitment, every child, every day. This was not framed as a career accelerant, but as a test of purpose.

Working in that context reinforced for me that mission-led leadership is rarely comfortable. It requires determination over time, a willingness to remain present when progress is uneven and a commitment to purpose even when the personal cost feels high. That experience has stayed with me, particularly in moments when it would have been easier to move on, soften focus or redefine success. Mission, when taken seriously, asks leaders not just to lead well, but to stay.

Determination is collective

Determination does not mean doing everything alone. Leaders who sustain purpose over time are those who draw on collective strength. They create structures for support, invite challenge and share responsibility. They recognise that resilience is not an individual trait but a relational one, built through trust, honesty and shared commitment.

Importantly, staying the course also involves knowing when to rest, pause or recalibrate. Determination without self-awareness can lead to burnout or disconnection. Leaders who remain effective over the long term are those who understand that care for self and care for mission are not competing priorities. Protecting energy, boundaries and perspective is part of the work, not a distraction from it.

In a system that often rewards immediacy and visibility, determination can be quiet and unglamorous. It shows up in consistent decision-making, in the willingness to revisit difficult conversations, and in the discipline to hold focus when distractions multiply. Over time, this steadiness becomes visible to others. It builds confidence, credibility and trust.

Research consistently highlights the relationship between sustained pressure, diminished autonomy and workforce attrition in education. Studies on teacher and leader wellbeing point to the cumulative impact of accountability, workload and emotional labour on retention, particularly when individuals feel they have limited control or support. While resilience is often emphasised, evidence suggests that cultures which prioritise clarity, trust and values-led decision-making are more likely to retain staff over time. This reinforces the importance of leadership approaches that protect both purpose and people.

Staying the course is not about resisting change. It is about ensuring that change remains connected to purpose. When leaders hold mission, strategy, autonomy and determination together, they create the conditions for progress that is both meaningful and sustainable. This work takes time. It requires patience, courage and the willingness to remain present even when the path forward is not immediately clear.

Accountability without losing yourself

Accountability as alignment vs accountability as fear

Accountability sits at the heart of educational leadership, yet it is one of the areas where leaders are most at risk of losing themselves. In a system shaped by inspection, performance measures and public scrutiny, accountability can easily become personal rather than professional, absorbed internally rather than held structurally.

At its best, accountability supports clarity, focus and improvement. It helps organisations remain aligned to purpose and ensures that actions have consequences. At its worst, accountability becomes synonymous with blame, fear and constant self-surveillance. Leaders begin to carry responsibility not just for outcomes, but for perceptions, judgements and narratives beyond their control.

The accumulation effect

One of the challenges for leaders is that accountability rarely arrives in neat, bounded forms. It accumulates. It is layered. Leaders are accountable upwards to regulators and governance, outwards to families and communities and inwards to staff and students. Without strong internal anchors, this weight can begin to distort decision-making. Leaders may prioritise what is most visible over what is most meaningful, or what is safest over what is right.

The slow loss of self

Losing yourself rarely happens in a single moment. It happens gradually, through small compromises made in the name of survival. Boundaries soften. Values are postponed. Decisions are justified rather than examined. Over time, leaders may find that they are performing leadership rather than practising it, meeting expectations while feeling increasingly disconnected from purpose.

Separate role from identity

Holding accountability without losing self requires intentional separation between *role* and *identity*. Leaders are responsible for decisions and outcomes, but they are not reducible to them. When accountability becomes fused with self-worth, leaders are more likely to over-function, avoid challenge or personalise critique. This not only damages wellbeing but weakens leadership judgement.

Values-led accountability offers an alternative. When leaders remain clear about mission and strategy, accountability can be reframed as alignment rather than threat. Questions shift from *How will this look?* to *Does this serve what we are here to do?* This does not remove pressure, but it changes how pressure is held.

Share the weight

Crucially, leaders who sustain themselves over time are those who do not carry accountability alone. They build structures that allow responsibility to be shared, challenges to be voiced and decisions to be tested collectively. They create spaces where uncertainty can be named and where accountability conversations are rooted in learning rather than fear.

Model accountability without shame

There is also an important relational dimension. Leaders who model healthy accountability make it possible for others to do the same. When mistakes are acknowledged openly, when decisions are explained honestly and when boundaries are held with care, accountability becomes something people engage with rather than resist. Trust grows not because leaders are infallible, but because they are consistent and transparent.

Accountability without losing yourself is not about lowering standards or avoiding scrutiny. It is about staying anchored. It is about recognising that leadership integrity is sustained through clarity, support and self-awareness. In complex systems, leaders will always be held to account. The question is not whether accountability exists, but whether it is held in a way that allows leaders and those they lead to remain human.

Leadership reflection: Holding the mission under pressure

Mission and strategy can feel deceptively stable when things are going well. Purpose is clear, direction feels shared and decisions align more easily with long-term intent. It is under pressure that mission is truly tested when urgency crowds out reflection, when competing demands pull attention in multiple directions and when leaders are asked to respond faster than they can think.

This reflection invites you to notice how mission shows up in your leadership *in practice*, not just in language. Many leaders do not consciously abandon purpose; instead, it becomes diluted through a series of small, reasonable decisions made in response to immediate pressures. Over time, this can lead to mission creep, where effort increases but focus narrows, and where leaders find themselves busy but disconnected from why the work matters.

The questions that follow are designed to help you reconnect strategy with values. Strategy is not about control or compliance; it is about creating the conditions for others to act with clarity and confidence. Authentic leadership requires holding mission steady while distributing responsibility, trusting others to exercise judgement and resisting the temptation to over-monitor when outcomes feel uncertain.

As you reflect, pay attention to where accountability strengthens purpose and where it may be eroding autonomy. Consider how determination shows up in your leadership, not as relentless endurance, but as the capacity to stay aligned, to say no when necessary and to return repeatedly to what matters most. Mission-led leadership is sustained not by doing more, but by doing what is meaningful with intention and care.

Take a moment to pause

This reflection invites you to consider how mission, strategy and accountability are shaping your leadership and how you are holding the weight of responsibility.

Reflect on mission

- How clear is your personal understanding of the mission you are serving right now?
- Where has that mission felt most alive in your recent decision-making?
- Where might it have become obscured by urgency or external pressure?

Reflect on strategy

- What strategic choices are you currently making that most clearly reflect your values?
- What are you choosing *not* to do, and how explicit are those choices to others?
- Where might overload or priorities accumulate without being checked, begin to dilute focus?

Reflect on autonomy and determination

- How much trust are you placing in others to exercise judgement aligned to purpose?
- Where are you holding on more tightly than necessary?
- What helps you stay the course when progress feels slow, or resistance emerges?

Reflect on accountability

- How do you experience accountability as alignment, threat or something else?
- Where might accountability be slipping into self-criticism rather than learning?
- What boundaries help you remain connected to purpose without absorbing everything personally?

Look ahead

- What is one decision you could approach with greater intentionality this week?
- Where might slowing down strengthen clarity rather than weaken momentum?
- What would it look like to lead accountably while protecting your integrity and wellbeing?

Mission-led leadership is sustained not through endurance alone, but through alignment, support and conscious choice.

References

Education Support. (2022). *Teacher Wellbeing Index 2022*. Education Support.

Fullan, M. (2014). *The Principal: Three Keys to Maximizing Impact*. Jossey-Bass.

National Foundation for Education Research (NFER). (2023). Teacher Labour Market in England Annual Report.

Schein, E. (2010). *Organizational Culture and Leadership* (4th ed.). Jossey-Bass.

6 No 'I' in team
Leading without losing yourself

Leadership in schools is often described as a collective endeavour, and rightly so. Research consistently highlights the importance of collaboration, trust and shared responsibility in effective organisations. Andy Hargreaves and Michael Fullan, for example, argue that strong professional cultures are built on collective efficacy rather than heroic individualism. Leadership, in this sense, is not about standing apart but about working together towards a shared moral purpose (Hargreaves & Fullan, 2012).

And yet, the lived experience of leadership can feel far more complex.

While teamwork is rightly celebrated, school leaders are often navigating unspoken expectations about harmony, consensus and self-sacrifice. The message can become subtly distorted: be collaborative, but don't disrupt; be relational, but don't challenge too hard; be part of the team, but carry the ultimate responsibility. For many leaders, particularly women and leaders from under-represented or global majority backgrounds, this tension is amplified. You are expected to belong, but not to unsettle; to contribute, but not to confront; to lead, but without appearing too forceful in doing so.

Kim Scott's work on *Radical Candour* reminds us that effective teams are built not on niceness, but on the ability to challenge directly while caring personally. Similarly, Patrick Lencioni highlights that the absence of trust is one of the most significant barriers to effective teamwork. Without trust, teams default to artificial harmony, a surface-level collegiality that avoids conflict but quietly erodes honesty and accountability (Lencioni, 2002; Scott, 2017).

This chapter explores that tension. How do leaders honour collaboration without losing clarity? How do they remain relational without becoming people-pleasers? And how do they lead as part of a team without losing themselves in the process?

Authentic leadership lives in that balance.

The myth of the hero leader

In (Chapter 10), I spoke about 'wearing the badge' and what that feels like, particularly when all eyes are on you. But there is something else that comes with

 DOI: 10.4324/9781003635666-6

wearing a leadership badge – something far more daunting, especially when you are appointed to a school in crisis, with an unspoken expectation that you will save the day.

On one level, that expectation feels understandable. After all, being appointed as a Deputy or Headteacher after a gruelling process is evidence that you can do the job. But should you and can you really be the hero who fixes everything, single-handedly?

Too often in schools, headteachers absorb a powerful narrative: that we should be heroic, endlessly resilient and willing to work tirelessly for our schools and communities. And many do. I certainly did. I found myself making decisions hourly, daily decisions that actually required deep thought, careful judgement and meaningful collaboration with my team. Yet, particularly in the early days of headship, I believed I had to arrive with all the answers. I was the Headteacher, how could I not?

Without realising it, I stepped into the role of the hero leader. I loved my job; there were no groans when the alarm went off at 6 am. But I was being emotionally and mentally drained. I was carrying everything. I was becoming the hero Headteacher, and it took its toll.

I can't count the hours I gave to the schools I worked in and led, often at the sacrifice of my own family. Once, a friend asked me how my girls were. I immediately began talking about the girls in my school, not my three daughters. It was a stark, uncomfortable moment. One that forced me to pause and reframe my leadership priorities.

That moment confronted me with a difficult truth: leadership was never meant to be a solo act. If I was exhausted, overwhelmed and quietly losing myself in the role, it wasn't because I cared too much; it was because I was trying to lead alone. And that is where the idea of teamwork becomes both necessary and complicated.

Collaboration isn't consensus

Collaboration is one of the most frequently used words in education. We champion it in staff briefings, build it into improvement plans and cite it as evidence of a healthy culture. Working together, we say, is the cornerstone of effective leadership. And yet, somewhere along the way, collaboration has become quietly conflated with agreement.

In many schools, collaboration can begin to mean keeping the peace. Meetings feel collegial on the surface, but difficult issues are softened, delayed or avoided altogether. Decisions are nodded through, not because everyone is convinced, but because nobody wants to be the one who disrupts the flow.

For leaders, this creates a particular tension. We are encouraged to be inclusive and relational, to listen carefully and bring people with us. But when collaboration becomes synonymous with consensus, leadership can lose its edge. Clarity gets diluted. Values become negotiable. And the very thing collaboration is meant to strengthen trust, begins to erode.

True collaboration is not about unanimous agreement or universal comfort. It is about collective responsibility, honest dialogue and the courage to surface different perspectives. It requires spaces where people can disagree respectfully, challenge ideas robustly and still remain connected to a shared purpose. Without that, collaboration risks becoming performative, something that looks good on paper but feels increasingly hollow in practice.

This is where authentic leadership matters most: in resisting the pull of artificial harmony and creating teams that can tell the truth, even when that truth is uncomfortable.

Moving beyond the hero: Creating conditions for collective leadership

In 2020, when I was awarded Headteacher of the Year, I felt overwhelmed, humbled and deeply grateful. Grateful for the wonderful staff, students, families and communities I had the privilege of working with. Grateful, too, for my leadership team for making me a better leader, for challenging me respectfully and for guiding me to make the right decisions for the school.

The thing about headship is that you are a Deputy on 31 August and a Headteacher on 1 September, and suddenly you are expected to have all the answers. But the truth is, people are sitting right in front of you who know far more than you do. The real leadership skill is recognising that and not feeling embarrassed to ask for their help.

David Marquet, a former US Navy submarine commander, offers a powerful reframing of leadership. He argues that greatness is not a personality trait lodged in the leader at the top, but a property of the system they create. Sustainable excellence depends not on the brilliance or heroics of one individual, but on whether the conditions exist for everyone to think, act and take responsibility (Marquet, 2016).

For schools, this is a vital lesson. When leaders stop positioning themselves as the answer, and instead redesign the environment so that others can lead, organisations become more resilient, more humane and more effective. This is seen in the confidence of staff to act without permission, in teams trusted to exercise professional judgement and in cultures where people are valued for contribution rather than compliance.

Trust, challenge and radical candour in practice

On one senior leadership team, I worked with an outstanding Deputy Headteacher and a Senior Assistant Headteacher who knew far more than I did when it came to data and Special Educational Needs and Disabilities. And that mattered. You need colleagues who understand legislation deeply, who can see risks and implications before they surface. The hero headteacher cannot – and should not – know it all.

There were times around the table when my Senior Assistant Headteacher would listen quietly before leaning in and saying, 'Evelyn, I'm not sure you've thought about x, y and z'.

My internal response, at least initially, was immediate: *I'm the Headteacher here.* But because we had built a culture of mutual respect, one where challenge was expected, and care was assumed, I knew this was a safe, constructive challenge.

This is what Kim Scott describes as Radical Candour: challenging directly while caring personally. It wasn't confrontational or performative. It was thoughtful, calm and rooted in a shared commitment to doing the right thing for the school.

Without her measured challenge, alongside the clarity and strength of my Deputy, I could easily have made decisions that left both the school and me in difficult territory. What this experience crystallised for me was the true value of teamwork: not agreement for its own sake, but the courage to challenge in service of shared values.

Emotional labour and the weight of expectation

One of the least visible aspects of leadership is emotional labour, the ongoing work of managing feelings, absorbing tension and holding space for others. In schools, this labour is often normalised. Leaders are expected to listen, reassure, de-escalate and remain composed, even when decisions are contested or emotions run high.

Being 'relational' can, over time, become shorthand for being endlessly available and accommodating. Leaders act as buffers, smoothing conflict so others do not have to. This work is rarely named and almost never shared.

What is less often acknowledged is that emotional labour is not neutral. Women, and leaders from global majority backgrounds, are often expected to be warmer, more patient and more accommodating. Assertiveness can be misread as aggression. Boundary-setting can be interpreted as aloofness. Over time, leaders learn to manage not just decisions, but how those decisions will *land*, who might feel unsettled and what emotional work will be required afterwards to repair the fallout.

This invisible labour is exhausting. It can quietly reshape leadership behaviour, encouraging avoidance over clarity and emotional containment over principled challenge. Authentic leadership requires us to name emotional labour for what it is: work. Relational leadership should not require self-erasure. Empathy does not mean avoidance. Protecting relationships should never come at the expense of integrity or self-trust.

Staying true to yourself inside the team

Belonging to a leadership team should not require self-betrayal. Yet in the name of collaboration, leaders can find themselves shelving concerns, softening language or second-guessing instincts until their values become harder to hear.

Staying true to yourself is not about ego or stubbornness. It is about integrity. It is noticing when something does not sit right and having the courage to say so, even when the room feels settled in another direction.

Over time, I have noticed certain signals that leaders may be losing themselves inside teams: rehearsing concerns but never voicing them; leaving meetings relieved rather than aligned; adding disclaimers such as 'I might be wrong, but...' before naming something important; or feeling responsible for everyone else's emotional response to clarity.

These are not signs of weakness. They are signs of empathy and care. But they are also invitations to pause. Psychological safety research reminds us that the most effective teams are not those without disagreement, but those where challenge is welcomed as contribution. Silence carries a cost. When leaders suppress their values to maintain harmony, teams lose an important moral compass (Edmondson, 2018).

When the team disagrees with you

In teams, values are not only tested by pressure, but my proximity, who others expect to align. There are moments when disagreement is immediate and deeply consequential. Behaviour decisions are a common example. On the surface, policy appears clear. A line has been crossed, and a consequence should follow. But leaders often hold information others do not: safeguarding context, family circumstances, trauma histories or wider system pressures.

To go against expectation can feel risky. It can feel like you are undermining policy, disappointing staff or exposing yourself to criticism. But authentic leadership is not rigid adherence to process; it is principled judgement.

What in these moments is clarity. Can you articulate *why* you are taking a different path? Can you hold discomfort without becoming defensive? Can you acknowledge disagreement while remaining anchored in your values?

Leading as part of a team does not mean outsourcing moral responsibility. Sometimes it means standing steady in tension and trusting that integrity will speak louder than agreement in the moment.

From team to culture

Leadership dynamics never stay contained within leadership rooms. Staff notice who speaks, who stays silent and how disagreement is handled. They notice whether challenge is welcomed or quietly shut down.

When leadership teams practise honest collaboration, that culture ripples outward. Trust becomes embedded not through policy, but through daily interactions. Conversely, when harmony is prioritised over honesty, cultures become brittle. Issues surface late, trust erodes quietly and compliance replaces contribution.

Leading without losing yourself is not about choosing between individuality and collaboration. It is about holding both with intention. There may be no 'I' in team, but there must always be integrity.

Leadership reflection: Leading with and within teams

Leadership can be an isolating experience, even within large organisations. Expectations, accountability and visibility can quietly pull leaders towards carrying responsibility alone, stepping in rather than stepping back and becoming the point where decisions, emotions and pressure collect. This reflection invites you to pause and consider how leadership is shared, supported and experienced within your teams.

The idea that strong leadership requires individual heroics is deeply embedded in many systems. Leaders are often praised for decisiveness, endurance and control, particularly in times of challenge. Yet authentic leadership is rarely about having all the answers. It is about creating the conditions where others feel able to think, challenge, contribute and lead alongside you. Teams thrive not when leaders do more, but when responsibility is distributed with trust and clarity.

The questions that follow are designed to help you notice where leadership may have become concentrated rather than collective. They invite reflection on power, emotional labour and psychological safety. Who feels able to challenge? Who carries invisible work? Who is protected and who absorbs pressure quietly? These dynamics shape team culture far more than formal structures alone.

As you reflect, consider where collaboration feels genuine and where it may be performative. Authentic leadership within teams requires humility, the willingness to listen and the confidence to allow others to lead differently from you. Letting go of control is not a loss of authority; it is an investment in capacity, trust and long-term sustainability.

Take a moment to pause

Leadership within teams often brings quiet pressures to be decisive, to carry responsibility or to hold everything together. This reflection invites you to consider how power, responsibility and collaboration show up in your leadership, and how your behaviour shapes the culture of the teams you lead.

Reflect on role and responsibility

- Where do you feel pressure to be the 'hero' rather than work collectively?
- How comfortable are you with sharing leadership, influence and credit?
- Where might your own sense of responsibility be limiting others' growth?

Strong teams rely on trust, not individual heroics.

Reflect on honesty and safety

- When have you prioritised harmony over honesty?
- How safe do people feel challenging you or offering a different perspective?
- What happens in your team when disagreement surfaces?

Psychological safety is built through everyday responses.

Reflect on fairness and emotional labour

- Where is emotional labour unevenly carried within your team?
- Who absorbs tension, conflict or additional responsibility without it being acknowledged?
- How intentional are you about noticing and addressing this?

Unseen labour shapes culture as much as formal roles.

Look ahead

- What values do you need to hold steady when team decisions feel contested?
- What one leadership behaviour could you adjust to strengthen collective responsibility and trust?

References

Edmondson, A. (2018). *The Fearless Organization.* Wiley.

Hargreaves, A., Fullan, M. (2012). *Professional Capital: Transforming Teaching in Every School.* Teachers College Press.

Lencioni, P. (2002). *The Five Dysfunctions of a Team.* Jossey-Bass.

Marquet, L. D. (2016). *Turn the Ship Around.* Portfolio.

Scott, K. (2017). *Radical Candor.* St. Martin's Press.

7 Trust and compassion
Why trust is not a soft skill

Trust is often spoken about in leadership as if it were a personality trait rather than a leadership outcome. We talk about being trustworthy, approachable or open, as though trust simply emerges from good intentions or warm relationships. In schools, trust is sometimes reduced to tone: being kind, being visible, being liked. But trust is not a soft skill. It is not incidental. And it is certainly not accidental.

Trust is built through behaviour

Trust is built or broken through leadership behaviour. Early in my headship, a coach shared a reminder I tried to hold onto: *trust takes years to build, seconds to break and far longer to repair*. Never is that more true than in high-pressure environments where priorities compete and scrutiny is constant.

In school communities, trust shows up long before it is named. It is present in those who feel able to speak honestly, who feel safe enough to challenge and who quietly disengage. It appears in staff rooms, in corridors, in meetings where some voices dominate, and others remain silent. Leaders rarely need to ask whether trust exists; they can observe it in patterns of behaviour, participation and presence.

What makes trust difficult is not that leaders do not value it, but that trust requires consistency under pressure. It is relatively easy to build trust when circumstances are calm, resources are available and decisions are popular. The real test comes when leaders must make difficult choices, hold boundaries or deliver messages that will not be welcomed. It is in those moments that trust is either strengthened or eroded.

This is why trust cannot be reduced to niceness. Being liked is not the same as being trusted. In fact, leaders who prioritise approval over clarity often weaken trust over time. When decisions feel inconsistent, unexplained or reactive, people begin to fill the gaps themselves. Silence grows. Cynicism creeps in. And trust, once fractured, becomes far harder to repair than it was to build.

Trust in leadership is rooted in predictability, not popularity. People trust leaders who do what they say they will do, who explain their reasoning even when the

DOI: 10.4324/9781003635666-7

answer is no and who act in ways that align with stated values. They trust leaders who are steady rather than performative, and who resist the temptation to shift position simply to ease discomfort in the moment.

Research consistently reinforces what many leaders experience instinctively: trust is not built through warmth alone, but through reliability, fairness and follow-through. Studies on psychological safety highlight that people are more likely to speak up, challenge decisions and remain engaged when leadership behaviour is predictable and explanations are transparent, even when decisions are unpopular. Trust, in this sense, is less about agreement and more about confidence in process. When leaders communicate clearly, act consistently and explain the reasoning behind their decisions, they reduce uncertainty and anxiety, particularly in high-pressure environments. Organisational research also suggests that trust functions as a form of social infrastructure, enabling collaboration, adaptability and resilience during periods of change. Without it, systems may still function on compliance, but they struggle to sustain commitment, innovation or discretionary effort over time.

Trust in relational systems

In education, trust carries particular weight because of the relational nature of the work. Schools are not transactional organisations. They are human systems built on interdependence, emotional labour and shared responsibility. Teachers, support staff, students and families all experience leadership decisions not just as policy, but as personal impact. When trust is present, people are more willing to stay engaged during periods of challenge. When it is absent, even well-intentioned initiatives can feel imposed rather than shared.

Trust under pressure

The past few years have made this painfully visible. During periods of uncertainty, whether driven by inspection pressure, staffing shortages or national crises, leaders have been required to make decisions without clear guidance or guaranteed outcomes. In those moments, trust has not been built through certainty, but through honesty.

Especially in the early days of headship, saying 'I don't yet have all the answers' can feel deeply uncomfortable. There is often a temptation to fill the space, to appear decisive or to offer reassurance that is not fully grounded. But as one experienced head once said to me, *blagging it might feel easier in the short term but in the long term, it does far more harm than good.* Trust is strengthened when leaders are willing to defer, to draw on collective expertise and to be honest about what they do and do not yet know.

This is where trust intersects with authenticity. Authentic leadership is not about transparency without boundaries, nor about sharing every emotion as it arises. It is about being real in ways that serve the community rather than the ego. Leaders who practise authentic communication, explaining the why behind decisions, acknowledging complexity and holding firm to values build trust even when agreement is not universal.

When trust erodes

It is also important to name what happens when trust is absent. In schools where trust has been eroded, leaders often encounter compliance without commitment. Policies are followed, but enthusiasm is thin. Innovation stalls. People do what is required, but no more. Over time, this creates brittle cultures that struggle to adapt or recover when further pressure is applied.

By contrast, trust-rich cultures are not conflict-free. Disagreement still exists, and decisions are still contested. The difference is how those tensions are carried. In high-trust environments, challenge is more likely to happen privately, constructively and with evidence. People feel confident that raising concerns will not lead to retribution or exclusion. Leaders are able to hear dissent without seeing it as a threat to authority.

When trust shapes retention

Trust also shapes retention. When staff feel trusted, trusted to exercise professional judgement, trusted to raise concerns, trusted to balance autonomy with accountability, they are more likely to stay, even when workload is heavy. When trust is missing, the emotional cost of staying often outweighs the professional rewards.

This is why trust must be understood as a leadership responsibility, not a cultural by-product. Leaders set the conditions in which trust can grow through their choices, their consistency and their willingness to explain rather than obscure. They model what trust looks like by how they handle pressure, how they respond to mistakes and how they treat people when outcomes are uncertain.

Trust is not built through grand gestures. It is built in ordinary moments: the decision to explain rather than dismiss, to listen rather than react, to act in alignment with values even when it would be easier not to. These moments accumulate. Over time, they create cultures where people feel safe enough to contribute, challenge and remain.

In this sense, trust is not soft at all. It is demanding. It requires discipline, self-awareness and restraint. It asks leaders to be clear rather than comforting, consistent rather than convenient and human without being uncontained.

Trust is the foundation on which compassionate leadership can stand, and without it, compassion risks being misunderstood as weakness rather than strength.

Compassion as discipline, not rescue

Compassion is one of the most misunderstood concepts in leadership.

In schools, it is often spoken about as a personal quality rather than a leadership practice. Compassion becomes associated with kindness, warmth or flexibility, valuable traits, but insufficient on their own. In pressured systems, compassion is sometimes framed as the opposite of rigour, accountability or ambition, as though leaders must choose between caring for people and delivering outcomes. This false dichotomy does real damage.

Compassion, when practised authentically, is not soft. It is disciplined. Research into compassionate leadership emphasises that compassion is most effective when paired with clarity, boundaries and accountability, particularly in complex systems where perceptions of fairness matter (West, 2021). Compassion without discipline can unintentionally create inconsistency, confusion or perceptions of unfairness, particularly in systems already under strain. Studies exploring equity in leadership practice highlight the distinction between treating people the same and responding to people according to their context and need. Compassion, when practised well, involves transparent decision-making, clear reasoning and an explicit connection to shared values. It requires leaders to explain not only *what* they have decided, but *why*, recognising that dignity is protected through understanding, even when outcomes differ. In this way, disciplined compassion supports trust, reduces resentment and sustains fairness, rather than undermining it.

Disciplined compassion requires leaders to hold people in mind without removing responsibility, to acknowledge difficulty without collapsing boundaries and to act with care even when decisions are unpopular. It is not about rescuing people from discomfort, but about supporting them to navigate it with dignity.

The rescue trap

One of the most common traps leaders fall into is equating compassion with accommodation. When staff are struggling, leaders may instinctively want to ease pressure by avoiding difficult conversations, delaying decisions or absorbing responsibility themselves. While this may feel caring in the moment, it often creates unintended consequences. Expectations become unclear. Resentment grows quietly. Emotional labour becomes unevenly distributed. Over time, this erodes trust rather than strengthens it.

Rescue is tempting because it offers immediate relief to others, and often to leaders themselves. But rescue is rarely sustainable. It positions the leader as the solution rather than the system, and it prevents honest conversations about capacity, workload or role boundaries. Compassionate leadership does not remove challenge; it helps people face challenge with clarity and support.

Disciplined compassion also requires leaders to think carefully about equity. In any school community, some staff, students or families will need something different in order to participate fully or to thrive. Responding to that difference is not favouritism; it is an act of professional judgement. However, without clarity and transparency, compassionate responses can easily be misunderstood by others as unfairness.

This is where leadership discipline matters. Compassionate leaders are intentional about explaining *why* flexibility is offered in some situations and not others, grounding those decisions in clear values rather than personal preference. Fairness, in this sense, is not about treating everyone the same, but about ensuring decisions are proportionate, principled and consistent with dignity. When leaders fail to articulate this, compassion risks being misread, not because it is wrong, but because it has not been made visible.

This distinction matters deeply in education, where emotional labour is constant and often invisible. Teachers and leaders routinely carry the weight of others' needs; students, families, colleagues, alongside their own. Compassion that lacks discipline risks asking leaders to carry more than is reasonable, while inadvertently signalling that boundaries do not matter. Over time, this can lead to burnout, resentment or withdrawal, particularly among those who are most committed.

Disciplined compassion, by contrast, recognises limits. It allows leaders to say, 'I care about this, and this is what I can and cannot do'. It involves explaining decisions, even when the answer is no. It means acknowledging the impact of those decisions, rather than hiding behind policy or process alone. When leaders take the time to explain their reasoning, they signal respect, and respect is a core component of compassionate practice.

This is where compassion intersects with clarity. Leaders who communicate clearly, even when delivering difficult messages, are often experienced as more compassionate than those who avoid discomfort. Clarity reduces uncertainty, and uncertainty is one of the greatest sources of anxiety in organisations. When people understand why decisions are made, they are more likely to accept outcomes, even when those outcomes are not what they hoped for.

Compassion also requires leaders to pay attention to patterns, not just moments. Supporting an individual repeatedly without addressing underlying structural issues may feel caring, but it can perpetuate the very pressures causing harm. Authentic compassion asks leaders to look beyond individual need and consider what systems are producing repeated strain. This is not a withdrawal of care, but an expansion of it.

Ultimately, compassion in leadership is not about protecting people from reality. It is about acknowledging reality honestly and responding in ways that preserve dignity. It is about recognising humanity without surrendering responsibility. When compassion is practised with discipline, it strengthens trust, sustains cultures and enables people to remain engaged even when the work is hard.

Compassion, then, is not an alternative to accountability. It is what makes accountability bearable, meaningful and just.

The human cost when trust is missing

When trust is missing, the impact is rarely immediate or dramatic. More often, it is gradual, quiet and cumulative.

In schools where trust has begun to erode, leaders may still see compliance. Policies are followed. Meetings are attended. Deadlines are met. But beneath the surface, something important has shifted. People begin to protect themselves. Questions go unasked. Concerns are softened or withheld entirely. Gradually, the space for honest dialogue narrows, and leadership begins to feel like something done *to* people rather than *with* them.

One of the earliest signs that trust is weakening is silence. Silence in meetings. Silence after decisions are made. Silence where curiosity or challenge once existed. This silence is often misread as agreement or professionalism, when in reality it may be a form of self-preservation. When people do not trust that raising concerns will lead to fair treatment or meaningful change, they adapt by disengaging.

I see this increasingly in my work with school and trust leaders who are new in post and seeking to establish trust after inheriting cultures that are deeply unsettled. They describe noticing that difficult conversations are no longer taking place in professional spaces. Concerns surface indirectly, escalate quickly or bypass line management altogether. This is not a sign of disloyalty or resistance; it is an indicator that trust has been damaged, and people no longer believe it is safe or worthwhile to speak openly.

The cost of this disengagement is human before it is organisational. Staff who no longer feel safe to speak honestly often carry stress privately. They replay conversations, second-guess decisions and manage uncertainty alone. Over time, this emotional labour takes its toll. Energy is diverted from teaching, collaboration and creativity towards coping and containment. The work still gets done, but at a personal cost that is rarely visible to leaders.

Trust breakdown also shapes how people interpret leadership behaviour. In low-trust environments, even neutral or well-intentioned decisions can be experienced as threatening or dismissive. Lack of explanation is filled with assumptions. Inconsistency is experienced as favouritism. Silence from leaders is interpreted as indifference. When trust is fragile, perception becomes reality, and leaders find themselves managing reaction rather than relationship.

This has particular consequences for those early in their careers. New teachers often arrive with enthusiasm, hope and a strong sense of purpose. When they encounter cultures where trust feels thin or conditional, the emotional dissonance can be profound. Many do not leave because the work is hard; they leave because the environment feels unsafe, unsupported or misaligned with their values.

The human cost of low trust is also felt unevenly. Those with less positional power, early career staff, support colleagues, or those from marginalised backgrounds, are often the first to withdraw. When trust is missing, people who already feel exposed or different are more likely to remain silent, comply outwardly and plan their exit quietly. In this way, trust erosion can deepen existing inequities, even when leaders have no intention of harming.

Evidence from across the education sector reinforces the connection between trust, wellbeing and retention. National workforce data and wellbeing research consistently highlight trust in leadership, psychological safety and perceived fairness as key factors influencing whether staff choose to stay (Education Support, 2022; NFER, 2023). Where trust is weak, staff are more likely to experience heightened stress, emotional exhaustion and disengagement, even when workload remains unchanged. Importantly, this research suggests that attrition is rarely driven by a single decision or policy; it is more often the cumulative effect of feeling unheard, unsupported or exposed over time. In this sense, trust is not a peripheral concern, but a central condition for sustaining people and protecting organisational capacity.

Leaders themselves are not immune to the effects of low trust. When leaders sense that honesty is risky or that decisions will be met with suspicion regardless of intent, they may become more guarded. Communication becomes more formal, more controlled and less relational. This, in turn, reinforces distance and fuels further mistrust. A cycle begins, often unintentionally, that is difficult to break without conscious intervention.

Trust loss also limits an organisation's capacity to respond to a challenge. In moments of crisis or rapid change, leaders rely on people to adapt, collaborate and problem-solve together. Where trust is weak, change initiatives are more likely to be met with resistance, fatigue or surface-level compliance. Where trust is strong, people are more willing to tolerate uncertainty, share responsibility and remain engaged even when outcomes are unclear.

It is important to say that trust is not lost because leaders make mistakes. Mistakes are inevitable in complex systems. Trust is lost when those mistakes are hidden, denied or handled defensively. Conversely, trust can be strengthened when leaders acknowledge missteps, explain decisions openly and demonstrate learning over time. Repair is possible, but it requires humility, consistency and patience.

The human cost of missing trust is not just measured in attrition figures or absence data. It is felt in diminished confidence, fractured relationships and the quiet erosion of purpose. People may stay physically present while emotionally disengaged. And when that happens, schools lose not only talent but the relational energy that sustains learning communities.

Recognising the human cost of low trust is not an exercise in blame. It is an invitation to notice what is happening beneath the surface, and to take responsibility for the conditions leaders create. Trust does not require perfection. It requires attention.

Where trust is rebuilt intentionally through explanation, fairness and care, people often re-engage. Conversations reopen. Energy returns. But this work must be done deliberately. Trust rarely repairs itself.

Understanding this human cost is essential because it clarifies why trust and compassion cannot be treated as optional leadership qualities. They are foundational to whether people feel able to remain, contribute and grow even when the work is demanding.

Holding authority without losing humanity

One of the persistent myths in leadership is that authority and humanity sit in tension with one another. To be taken seriously, leaders must distance themselves emotionally; to be compassionate, they must somehow loosen their grip on standards, expectations or control. This belief is particularly strong in schools, where leaders operate under constant scrutiny and feel pressure to appear decisive, composed and unshakeable.

In reality, authority is not weakened by humanity. It is strengthened by it.

Authority in leadership is not rooted in position alone. While titles confer responsibility, they do not automatically generate trust or confidence. Authority is built relationally, through credibility, consistency and the way leaders conduct themselves under pressure. Leaders who are able to remain calm, reflective and grounded are often experienced as more authoritative than those who rely on distance or rigidity.

The confusion often arises when humanity is mistaken for emotional disclosure. Being human in leadership does not mean sharing every feeling or uncertainty as it arises. It does not require leaders to offload emotion onto others or to seek reassurance from those they are meant to support. Instead, it involves emotional regulation, the ability to notice what you are feeling, to manage it responsibly and to communicate in ways that are steady and purposeful.

This distinction matters. Leaders who practise emotional regulation create a sense of safety around them. They model how to remain composed without becoming cold, and how to care without becoming overwhelmed. In moments of difficulty, their steadiness becomes a form of leadership in itself. People may not agree with every decision, but they are more likely to trust the process by which those decisions are made.

Emotional regulation, however, should not be confused with emotional suppression. Showing emotion is not a failure of leadership; it is often a reminder of our shared humanity. There are moments when allowing emotion to be visible reinforces connection rather than undermining authority.

Research into leadership and emotional regulation highlights the role leaders play in shaping the emotional climate of their organisations, with calm, attuned leadership behaviour associated with greater psychological safety and clearer thinking under pressure (Goleman, 2013). Emotional regulation does not require emotional suppression; rather, it involves managing intensity and timing so that emotion supports understanding rather than overwhelms it. Studies exploring leadership presence and psychological safety suggest that calm, attuned leadership behaviour reduces anxiety, supports trust and enables clearer thinking during moments of uncertainty or crisis. In this way, emotional regulation becomes a relational skill, one that allows leaders to remain human while providing steadiness for others.

I have referred to the pandemic several times throughout this book, partly because of the decisions leaders were required to make, but also because of the emotional weight those moments carried. I remember the first government announcement to close schools and calling an emergency assembly for Year 11 to explain that they would be going home, that their prom and leavers' assembly would not take place. I was tearful. I tried to hold it back, but it was hard because I knew how deeply upsetting this would be for them. These moments mark rites of passage, and that loss mattered.

Did I think this made me a weak leader? No. Was I momentarily self-conscious that staff and students saw me in tears? Perhaps. But I also knew that suppressing emotion entirely does damage too. What matters is not the absence of feeling but the leader's ability to hold emotion responsibly to remain present, clear and focused on those they serve, even while feeling themselves deeply.

Holding authority also requires clarity. Leaders who explain decisions clearly, even when those decisions are unpopular, are often experienced as more legitimate than those who avoid explanation. Clarity does not remove disappointment, but it reduces confusion. It signals respect. When leaders take the time to articulate reasoning, constraints and values, they demonstrate that authority is being exercised thoughtfully rather than arbitrarily.

This is particularly important when leaders must say no. Refusing a request, setting a boundary or enforcing a standard can feel uncomfortable, especially for leaders who value relationships. But when no is communicated with care and explanation, it does not diminish authority; it reinforces it. People may not like the outcome, but they are more likely to accept it when they understand the why.

Authority is also shaped by how leaders respond to challenge. Leaders who are secure in their role are better able to hear dissent without perceiving it as a threat. They do not need to shut down disagreement to maintain control. Instead, they can invite challenge privately, engage with evidence and make decisions without humiliating or marginalising those who raise concerns. This approach signals confidence, not weakness.

Conversely, leaders who rely on positional authority alone often find themselves needing to assert it more frequently. Control becomes louder. Communication becomes more directive. As this continues, it can create distance and defensiveness, particularly in environments already under strain. What is lost in these moments is not just goodwill, but the relational foundation that makes leadership sustainable.

Holding authority without losing humanity also requires leaders to be conscious of visibility. People watch closely how leaders behave when things go wrong, when mistakes are made or when pressure mounts. Leaders who are able to acknowledge missteps without becoming defensive, and who demonstrate learning rather than blame, model a form of authority that is credible and grounded. They show that strength and humility are not opposites.

In practice, this kind of authority allows leaders to make difficult decisions without becoming isolated. It enables them to remain connected to the people they lead, even as responsibility increases. And it creates cultures where authority is understood not as dominance, but as stewardship, a responsibility to use influence wisely, fairly and with care.

Holding authority, then, is not about hardening oneself against emotion or complexity. It is about developing the capacity to remain present, clear and humane in the midst of it. Leaders who manage to do this consistently are often those who command the deepest trust, not because they are flawless, but because they are dependable.

What leaders owe the people they lead

Leadership carries authority, but it also carries obligation.

Leaders shape far more than strategy, systems or outcomes. Through their decisions, behaviours and patterns of response, they shape how safe people feel, how willing they are to speak and whether they believe their contribution matters. Trust and compassion are not abstract values in this context; they are experienced daily through leadership practice.

At its core, leadership owes people clarity. Not certainty, and not perfection, but honesty about what is known, what is still unfolding and how decisions will be made. In complex environments, clarity becomes an act of care. It reduces anxiety, prevents speculation and helps people orient themselves even when outcomes are uncertain.

Leadership also owes people fairness. This does not mean treating everyone the same, but acting with consistency, transparency and proportionality. When people understand the principles guiding decisions, even difficult ones, trust is more likely to be held. Fairness reassures communities that leadership is not arbitrary, reactive or driven by favour.

Leaders also owe people dignity. Dignity is upheld when conversations happen respectfully, when concerns are taken seriously and when accountability is exercised without humiliation or avoidance. It is upheld when leaders remember that impact matters as much as intention, and that how decisions are carried can either preserve or erode trust.

Importantly, leaders do not owe people the removal of all discomfort. Challenge, change and accountability are part of any meaningful work. What leaders do owe is the commitment to hold those moments with care to stay present, regulated and grounded in values, even when the work is hard.

Trust and compassion are sustained through ordinary, repeated choices. The decision to explain rather than dismiss. To listen rather than react. To act in alignment with values rather than expedience. Over time, these choices accumulate into cultures where people feel safe enough to remain, to contribute and to challenge when it matters most.

This is not easy work. It asks leaders to notice themselves as much as they notice others, and to remain attentive even when pressure mounts. But when trust and compassion are held together with clarity and accountability, leadership becomes not just something that is exercised, but something that is experienced, as fair, human and dependable.

It is from this place that leaders are best able to stay in the conversations that matter most.

Leadership reflection: Trust and compassion in practice

Trust and compassion are often discussed as ideals, but they are experienced most clearly in moments of pressure, disagreement or uncertainty. This reflection is not an evaluation of whether you are a 'trusting' or 'compassionate' leader. It is an invitation to notice the conditions you create around you, particularly when the work is demanding, and the stakes feel high.

Leaders often assume that trust is present until it is challenged. In reality, trust is revealed through patterns of behaviour: how decisions are explained, how disagreement is handled, how mistakes are responded to and how consistently values are upheld. Compassion, too, is not defined by intention alone. It is experienced through clarity, boundaries, fairness and the willingness to engage honestly rather than avoid discomfort.

These questions are designed to slow you down. Not to create hesitation, but to create awareness. Authentic leadership requires the courage to look closely at how others experience our leadership, especially when that experience may not fully align with how we see ourselves. Reflection is not about self-criticism; it is about responsibility. It allows leaders to notice small shifts that can strengthen trust, protect dignity and sustain relationships over time.

As you reflect, resist the urge to answer quickly or defensively. Sit with what feels uncomfortable or unresolved. The aim is not to reach certainty, but to deepen understanding. Trust and compassion are not traits you either have or lack; they are practices you return to, again and again, particularly when leadership feels most exposed.

Take a moment to pause

Trust and compassion are easy to endorse in principle, but far more demanding to practise consistently. This reflection invites you to consider how your leadership behaviour shapes trust, particularly under pressure.

Reflect on trust

- When was the last time someone disagreed with you openly? What helped make that possible?
- How confident are you that concerns would be raised directly with you rather than elsewhere?
- Where might silence be signalling self-protection rather than agreement?

Trust is revealed not by words, but by behaviour over time.

Reflect on compassion

- How do you distinguish between compassion and rescue in your leadership practice?
- When have you held a boundary while still preserving dignity?
- Are there situations where your desire to be kind may have delayed necessary clarity?

Compassion without clarity can unintentionally erode trust.

Reflect on fairness and equity

- Where do different people in your community need different forms of support?
- How do you explain those decisions, so they are experienced as fair rather than arbitrary?
- What principles guide your judgement when flexibility is required?

Fairness is not sameness, but transparency and consistency.

Reflect on accountability

- How comfortable are you holding others to account with honesty and care?
- What happens when accountability feels uncomfortable, do you lean in or pull away?
- How do you model accountability in your own leadership behaviour?

Trust grows when accountability is exercised with integrity.

Look ahead

- What is one leadership behaviour you could strengthen that would build trust more intentionally?
- Where might greater clarity, rather than greater comfort, serve your community better?
- How will you ensure that trust and compassion remain visible, especially when pressure increases?

Trust and compassion are sustained through ordinary choices, repeated with intention.

References

Education Support. (2022). *Teacher Wellbeing Index 2022.* Education Support.

Goleman, D. (2013). The focused leader. *Harvard Business Review, 91*(12), 50–60.

National Foundation for Educational Research (NFER). (2023). *Teacher Labour Market in England Annual Report 2023.* NFER.

West, M. (2021) *Compassionate Leadership.* Teacher Labour Market in England Annual Report 2023. National Foundation for Education Research.

8 Necessary conversations
Accountability as an act of care

As a leader, you will inevitably find yourself engaging in conversations with staff, students, governors or parents that make your heart sink. Nobody enjoys moments that are uncomfortable, tense or emotionally charged, especially when you know the conversation in front of you may be life-changing for the person on the receiving end. Yet this is the reality of school leadership. It comes with the badge. It comes with responsibility. And, quietly but importantly, it comes with the privilege of serving others well.

Throughout my career, I worked hard to reframe these moments. I stopped referring to them as *difficult conversations* and began to think of them as *necessary conversations*. That shift mattered. Necessary conversations honour the truth. They acknowledge humanity. And when handled well, they leave the person walking out of your office not diminished or ashamed, but with their dignity intact and their belief in themselves and in you preserved.

This chapter is grounded in one central belief: holding people to account, when done with dignity and care, is not a failure of kindness, but one of its clearest expressions.

That belief became my benchmark.

I often entered these conversations asking myself a simple but grounding question: *How would I want to be treated if I were sitting in that chair?* I remembered moments in my own career when feedback had been delivered in ways that were humiliating, abrupt or careless, and I reminded myself: *Don't become that leader. Don't replicate that harm.*

Respect over popularity

Necessary conversations from leaders

I have written elsewhere about the challenges I faced when I became a headteacher, and how leading with authenticity meant I was not always liked. I was not always supported. But in most cases, I was respected. And there is an important distinction there that we do not talk about enough in leadership.

 DOI: 10.4324/9781003635666-8

You can be disliked for a decision and still respected for the way you deliver it.

Susan Scott reminds us that 'the conversation *is* the relationship'. I agree, but in schools, that relationship exists within a deeply human ecosystem. Schools are not corporate environments; they are relational communities. Conversations ripple. Words linger. And every necessary conversation becomes a moment of leadership formation, not performative, but formative (Scott, 2004).

How you handle it tells people who you are.

The language shift: From 'difficult' to 'necessary'

Words shape mindset. When we label a conversation as *difficult*, we brace ourselves for conflict. Our shoulders tense. Our tone hardens. We enter the room prepared to defend or to be defended against.

But when we name it a *necessary conversation*, the purpose changes. A necessary conversation is rooted in care. It says: *This matters. You matter. Our students matter. And this is too important to ignore.*

Leaning in calmly, purposefully and compassionately is leadership at its best.

Accountability is kindness

This is the point where many leaders feel uneasy.

In training sessions with middle leaders, I am often asked how to balance being *kind* with holding people to account. The underlying fear is familiar: *If I challenge this, will I damage the relationship? If I push here, will I be seen as unkind?*

The truth is this: the greater damage is done when issues are left unaddressed, and expectations remain unclear.

Avoiding accountability does not protect people.

It leaves them stuck.

It leaves others carrying the weight.

And it leaves students exposed to inconsistency.

Accountability, when rooted in care, is not punishment; it is belief. It says: *I believe you are capable of better, and I care enough not to look away.*

Niceness that avoids truth is not kindness; it is comfort-seeking. Leadership that prioritises comfort over clarity ultimately fails the very people it claims to protect.

Clarity is kindness.

Consistency is kindness.

Following through is kindness.

When leaders avoid necessary conversations

The cost of silence

Avoidance is one of the most seductive traps in leadership. It often disguises itself as kindness, patience or emotional intelligence. Leaders tell themselves they are 'giving it time', 'choosing their battles' or 'not wanting to make things worse'. But in schools, avoidance is rarely neutral. It is a decision and one with consequences.

When necessary conversations are delayed or avoided altogether, the issue rarely disappears. More often, it mutates. What began as a manageable concern becomes a source of resentment, confusion or quiet disengagement. Standards slip unevenly. Inconsistencies multiply. And the emotional labour is redistributed – usually onto those who are already carrying the most.

Avoidance does not protect relationships; it corrodes them.

Avoidance is also deeply destabilising for belonging. People need clarity to feel safe. When expectations are vague or inconsistently enforced, individuals are left guessing where they stand. Silence breeds anxiety. People begin to read meaning into what is not said.

Leaders often avoid necessary conversations not out of kindness, but out of fear, fear of being disliked, fear of conflict, fear of getting it wrong. But leadership is not about waiting until fear disappears. It is about acting responsibly *in spite* of it.

Avoidance models something dangerous. When leaders do not name issues directly, others learn to speak sideways instead. Frustration is shared in corridors rather than conversations. Over time, politeness replaces honesty, and when it suppresses truth, it is rarely kind.

Necessary conversations are acts of stewardship. They say: *This matters too much to ignore.*

Power, positional authority and ethical use of influence

Every necessary conversation takes place within an imbalance of power. Titles matter. Decisions carry weight. Futures can be shaped by what is said and by how it is said. Ignoring this reality does not make leadership more humane; it makes it less honest.

Power amplifies everything. A casual comment can feel crushing. A poorly timed question can land as an accusation. Tone, posture and pauses are all read through the lens of authority.

Ethical leadership requires discipline. It asks leaders to regulate themselves, not just others. To notice whether they are seeking resolution or release. To ask: *Am I using my position to help this person grow, or to relieve my own frustration?* This does not mean diluting expectations. Used well, power creates clarity and safety. Used poorly, it breeds fear and silence. Leadership is not about saying everything you know. It is about discernment, knowing what needs to be addressed, when, and how.

Necessary conversations reveal how leaders understand their power. They show whether authority is being used to control or to care, to diminish or to develop. When used ethically, accountability feels like structure. It feels like safety. It feels like belonging (Edmondson, 2018).

The anatomy of a necessary conversation

Necessary conversations are not single events; they are processes. They require intention, emotional intelligence and courage, not loud or performative courage, but the quiet kind that holds compassion and firmness together. Before we engage in a necessary conversation, following these simple steps is likely to result in the outcome you are looking for:

Prepare yourself. Data matters, but emotional posture matters more. Pause. Ground yourself. Preparation is an act of respect.

Create safety before clarity. People cannot hear the truth if they feel threatened. Safety does not remove accountability; it enables it.

Speak honestly, with compassion. You do not soften the truth; you soften the landing. Focus on behaviour, impact and possibility.

Listen with curiosity. Silence can be powerful. Understanding reduces defensiveness.

Co-construct the way forward. Without a plan, a necessary conversation becomes just another difficult one.

Protect dignity. Always. No gossip. No retelling. What is shared is held with care.

What this looks like in practice

I once worked with a member of staff, I'll call her *A*, who was widely respected for her commitment to students. She arrived early, stayed late and cared deeply about the children in her lessons. But over time, something began to slip. Lessons became inconsistent. Behaviour issues escalated. Planning was rushed. The passion was still there, but the impact was no longer what it needed to be.

But the longer the issue went unaddressed, the heavier the atmosphere became.

When the necessary conversation finally happened, *A* arrived visibly anxious. Her body language suggested she was bracing for judgement. The conversation began not with accusation, but with clarity.

'This isn't about effort', I said. 'It's about impact. And right now, the impact isn't where it needs to be'.

There was a pause. Then tears, not because the feedback was cruel, but because it was honest. For the first time, *A* felt seen not just as someone who cared, but as someone who was struggling. What followed was not a list of failings, but a shared exploration: what was getting in the way, what support was missing and what success would look like again. Expectations were named clearly. Support was agreed explicitly. A timeline was set.

Crucially, I followed up, not to monitor, but to check in.

Over the following weeks, confidence began to return. Practice improved. Behaviour stabilised. But perhaps more importantly, *A* later reflected that the conversation had been a turning point:

> I thought saying something meant you'd given up on me. I realise now it meant the opposite.

This is what accountability looks like when it is rooted in care. Not rescue. Not avoidance. But belief, made visible through action.

When I got it wrong and why repair matters

I would be misleading if I suggested I always got this right.

There were moments when exhaustion and pressure bled into my tone. I remember one conversation where I spoke too quickly, interrupted too often and failed to leave space. The feedback was not wrong, but the delivery stripped dignity. The next day, I apologised. No justification. No ego. Repair did not weaken my leadership; it strengthened it.

You cannot lead authentically if you cannot apologise. Repair is leadership.

Students, parents and necessary conversations

The same principles apply with even greater care when necessary conversations involve students and parents. For students, these moments shape identity. Accountability must communicate: *this behaviour is not acceptable; I believe you can do better; and I will support you to get there.* Parents often arrive carrying fear, frustration or shame. Schools hold symbolic power. And for some communities in particular who feel that school failed them, this power imbalance can be felt even more profoundly. What is therefore needed is clear, compassionate communication which builds trust even when the message is hard.

Avoidance with families deepens misunderstanding. Silence creates narratives. Thoughtful engagement, even when uncomfortable, is often the most respectful path.

Necessary conversations with students and parents are not about winning arguments. They are about safeguarding relationships while upholding values.

Handled well, they communicate: *we care enough to tell the truth, and we care enough to do it well.*

A necessary conversation with a family

A Year 9 student had been repeatedly removed from lessons for disruptive behaviour. Each incident was logged. Letters were sent home. Sanctions escalated. Yet nothing changed. The behaviour continued, and the relationship between school and home grew increasingly strained. When the parent finally came in for a meeting, they arrived defensive and angry. Past experiences of education had left them mistrustful, and they were ready for confrontation.

The leader began by naming the reality without judgement. 'I want to be clear about the behaviour, it goes against our school values, it isn't acceptable and it can't continue. But I also want to understand what's sitting underneath it'. That sentence changed the temperature of the room, and as the conversation unfolded, it became clear that the student was struggling with anxiety and masking it through disruption. No one had previously asked *why* only *what.*

The expectations remained firm. Boundaries were not softened. But the way forward was reframed as a partnership rather than a punishment. Support was agreed. Communication channels were clarified. The student was spoken to directly, with dignity, not shame. Weeks later, the parent said something that stayed with the leader: 'This is the first time school hasn't made us feel like we're the problem'.

Necessary conversations with families are remembered not for the policies cited, but for the respect shown. Accountability, when paired with dignity, builds trust even in moments of conflict.

Necessary conversations and belonging

As explored in Chapter 4 on Belonging, cultures are shaped not by what we claim to value, but by what people experience day after day. Necessary conversations sit at the intersection of belonging and accountability.

Belonging is not about comfort.

It is about clarity, connection and care.

Avoidance erodes belonging. Necessary conversations, done well, strengthen it.

The cultural ripple

When leaders handle necessary conversations with dignity and clarity, the impact extends far beyond the individuals involved. It shapes culture. It lowers the emotional cost of honesty. Middle leaders replicate what they see. Issues surface earlier. Trust deepens, and even students notice. They learn how adults disagree, challenge and repair.

A healthy school is not one without conflict. It is one where conflict is handled with care.

Leadership reflection: Staying in the conversation

Necessary conversations are rarely avoided because leaders do not care. More often, they are avoided because leaders care deeply about relationships, about morale, about being fair and about the consequences of getting it wrong. This reflection invites you to pause and notice not just the conversations you have had, but the ones you may be carrying quietly and repeatedly postponing.

Avoidance often presents itself as patience, kindness or pragmatism. Leaders tell themselves they are waiting for the right moment, gathering more evidence or protecting others from discomfort. Sometimes this is true. But over time, avoidance can begin to erode trust, clarity and accountability. What remains unsaid does not disappear; it is felt in tension, uncertainty and diminished confidence.

The questions that follow are not about delivering difficult messages more forcefully. They are about holding both truth and dignity at the same time. Authentic leadership requires the courage to name what needs to change while communicating care for the person involved. It asks leaders to stay present in discomfort, rather than rushing to resolution or withdrawing entirely.

As you reflect, consider how people typically experience you in moments of challenge. Not just what you say, but how you say it. Notice where silence may be communicating more than words. Necessary conversations are not a failure of leadership; they are an expression of it. When handled with clarity, respect and consistency, they strengthen relationships rather than damage them. Staying in the conversation is not about being fearless; it is about being responsible.

Take a moment to pause

These reflections invite you to consider not whether conversations are difficult, but how you choose to stay present when they are.

Reflect on avoidance and impact

- Think about a conversation you may be avoiding right now. What has stopped you from having it?
- What message does avoidance send to the person involved and to others watching?
- How does avoidance shape trust, clarity or culture over time?

Avoidance is not neutral. It always communicates something.

Reflect on how conversations are experienced

- How do people usually feel after a necessary conversation with you?
- Do your words hold both truths: *this must change,* and *you still matter*?
- How intentional are you about tone, timing and setting when addressing difficult issues?

Necessary conversations are remembered less for what was said and more for how they were carried.

Reflect on courage and accountability

- When was the last time you stayed in a conversation even when it felt uncomfortable?
- Where might clarity be kinder than silence?
- What does compassionate accountability look like in your context?

Courageous leadership is not harsh; it is honest and humane.

Look ahead

- What one small action will you take this week to model courageous, compassionate accountability?
- How will you prepare yourself to stay present in the conversation rather than retreat from it?

References

Edmondson, A. (2018). *The Fearless Organiszation: Creating Psychological Safety in the Workplace for Learning, Innovation and Growth. Wiley.*

Scott, S. (2004). *Fierce Conversations: Achieving Success at Work and in Life One Conversation at a Time.* Berkley Books.

9 This is how it's done

Up to this point, this book has explored *why* authentic leadership matters: the lived experiences that shape us, the pressures that distort us and the values that keep us grounded. It has examined belonging, trust, teamwork, visibility and the emotional weight of leadership in schools today.

What comes next is different.

This chapter marks a shift from reflection to application, from narrative to practice. Not because leadership can be reduced to a set of instructions, but because leaders deserve more than reassurance alone. They deserve clarity about how authenticity shows up when the stakes are high, the answers are unclear and the responsibility is ultimately theirs.

Authentic leadership is often spoken about in abstract terms: integrity, empathy, courage, values. But school leaders do not lead in abstraction. They lead in real time, under pressure, with incomplete information, competing demands and consequences that affect real people. The question is not *whether* leadership is complex; it is how we navigate that complexity without losing ourselves, our teams or our moral compass.

This chapter is not about doing leadership perfectly. It is about doing it *honestly*. It is about the daily decisions that shape culture, the conversations that test values and the moments where leaders must choose between what is easy and what is right. It is written for leaders who want to act with integrity in imperfect systems and who are willing to accept that authenticity is not a destination, but a discipline.

What follows is not a blueprint. It is a set of anchors: ways of thinking, deciding and showing up that help leaders stay grounded when certainty is unavailable. This is how authentic leadership is lived, not in theory, but in practice.

The anchors of practice

Values-led decision-making in real time

One of the hardest adjustments leaders make is accepting that many of the most important decisions will never feel tidy. There will be no perfect option, no clear

 DOI: 10.4324/9781003635666-9

consensus and no solution that leaves everyone satisfied. Yet these are often the moments when leadership matters most.

In schools, decision-making is frequently presented as a technical exercise: policy followed, process applied, outcome delivered. And yet, on any given day, schools are interacting and interfacing with hundreds, sometimes thousands of individuals, children and adults alike, each bringing their own histories, hopes, vulnerabilities and challenges. I genuinely believe there is no other organisation quite like it. Schools are moral, relational, emotional and public spaces all at once. The idea that leadership decisions in such environments can ever be purely technical is a misunderstanding of the work itself (Fullan, 2014).

Lived leadership, therefore, is rarely straightforward. Decisions about behaviour, exclusion, safeguarding, staffing, resource allocation or parental challenge often sit at the intersection of competing pressures. What feels fair may not feel kind. What appears consistent may not feel humane. What seems compassionate in the short term may carry longer-term consequences that are far harder to bear. Leaders are constantly navigating trade-offs, not absolutes.

Leaders can feel intense pressure to appear certain. To act quickly. To communicate confidence, even when they are still weighing the implications of a decision. Early in leadership roles, it is easy to absorb the belief that decisiveness equals competence and hesitation equals weakness. In high-accountability systems, uncertainty can feel dangerous, something to be hidden rather than acknowledged. Over time, however, many leaders learn the opposite: that some of the most responsible decisions require pause, consultation and the courage to sit with uncertainty before acting (Heifetz et al., 2009).

Values-led decision-making does not remove ambiguity; it gives leaders something stable to return to when clarity is unavailable. Policies, procedures and frameworks are essential; they provide structure, consistency and protection, but they cannot anticipate every context or complexity. Leaders are therefore required to interpret policy through a human lens, holding both the letter and the spirit of what the school stands for. This interpretive work is not a deviation from professionalism; it is one of its most demanding expressions.

This is where leadership becomes deeply personal.

Every leader brings their own values, experiences and moral compass into the role, whether consciously or not. Decisions resonate differently depending on who you are, what you have lived and what you carry with you. The longer you lead, the more you realise that some decisions stay with you long after they are made, not because they were wrong, but because they mattered.

There are moments when you will know more than those around the table. I have given an example earlier in the book in relation to behaviour, but this shows up repeatedly in senior leadership. As a Headteacher or senior leader, you may be holding safeguarding information, contextual detail or strategic considerations that cannot be fully shared. From the outside, a decision may appear obvious. From the inside, it may feel anything but. In those moments, leadership can feel isolating, not because you are unwilling to listen, but because responsibility ultimately sits with you.

The three default reactions under pressure

When there is no perfect answer, leaders often default to one of three responses. Some retreat into policy, using it as a shield against challenge or discomfort. Policy becomes a way of closing down discussion rather than guiding judgement. Others lean heavily into empathy, avoiding decisions that may cause upset, even when clarity and firmness are required. Compassion becomes avoidance. A third response is speed, deciding quickly to escape the discomfort of not knowing, mistaking urgency for effectiveness.

Values-led leadership asks different questions.

Instead of asking, 'What will cause the least pushback?', it asks, 'What aligns most closely with who we say we are?'

Instead of asking, 'What is the safest option for me?', it asks, 'What is the most responsible option for the children and community we serve?'

These questions do not make decisions easier, but they make them more honest. They slow leaders down in productive ways. They create space for judgement rather than reaction. And they help leaders act with integrity even when certainty is unavailable.

Importantly, values-led decisions are not made in isolation. Authentic leaders seek counsel, not confirmation. They invite challenge, listen carefully and test their thinking against others' perspectives. This is not a sign of uncertainty; it is a recognition that wisdom rarely sits with one person alone. Strong leaders know when to listen widely and when to take responsibility for the final call.

Explain the why, not just the what

There will be times when you go against prevailing opinion, sometimes even within your own team. These moments require particular care. Explaining *why* a decision has been made matters as much as the decision itself. People may not agree, but they are more likely to trust leaders who are transparent about their reasoning, honest about constraints and clear about the values guiding their judgement. Silence or defensiveness in these moments often causes more damage than the decision itself.

This is especially true when decisions carry emotional weight. Exclusions, staffing restructures, safeguarding actions or high-stakes parental complaints leave a residue. Leaders feel this, even when they do not show it. Authentic leadership does not demand emotional detachment; it demands emotional responsibility. It allows leaders to acknowledge the impact of decisions on others and on themselves without becoming paralysed by it.

Over time, experienced leaders come to accept that some decisions will never feel fully resolved. Reflection, hindsight and external commentary will always offer alternative interpretations. What sustains leaders is not the illusion of perfection, but the discipline of consistency returning again and again to their values, their purpose and their responsibility to act with integrity.

When there is no perfect answer, values become a compass rather than a rulebook. They do not eliminate doubt, but they prevent drift. They help leaders remain grounded when pressure is high, voices are loud and certainty is scarce.

This is where authentic leadership begins in practice: not in having the right answer, but in making the most responsible one you can, with care, courage and clarity.

Accountability without fear

Holding the line without breaking people

Accountability is one of the most misunderstood aspects of leadership in schools. It is often framed as something that must be enforced tightly, uncompromisingly and unforgivingly, particularly in high-pressure environments where results, inspections and external scrutiny loom large. In these contexts, accountability can quickly slide into fear: fear of getting it wrong, fear of consequences, fear of being seen to fail.

Yet fear is a poor foundation for sustained improvement.

Authentic leadership reframes accountability not as punishment, but as responsibility to children, to colleagues and to the shared purpose of the organisation. At its best, accountability is about clarity and care, working together. It is about being explicit about expectations, honest about performance and committed to improvement, while still recognising the humanity of the people involved.

This balance matters because fear-based accountability may produce short-term compliance, but it erodes trust over time. When people are afraid, they narrow their focus. They become cautious rather than curious, defensive rather than reflective. They protect themselves, stop taking risks, stop speaking honestly and stop learning. In schools, the consequences of this are significant: innovation stalls, professional judgement is sidelined and cultures become brittle rather than resilient.

Accountability without fear starts with clarity. Ambiguity creates anxiety, and anxiety fuels defensiveness. When expectations are unclear, feedback feels personal rather than professional and challenge feels arbitrary rather than purposeful. Leaders who are explicit about standards, roles and responsibilities reduce uncertainty and create safer conditions for honest dialogue. Clarity, delivered calmly and consistently, is not harshness; it is an act of care.

This clarity also requires leaders to separate behaviour from identity. Saying 'this is not good enough' is very different from saying 'you are not good enough'. One invites growth; the other triggers protection. Skilled leaders are precise in their language, addressing actions, impact and expectations rather than making assumptions about intent or worth. This precision protects dignity while still holding standards.

It is in necessary conversations that this distinction matters most. Avoiding challenge in the name of kindness often leads to greater harm in the long run. Issues remain unaddressed. Resentment builds quietly. Teams lose confidence in leadership's willingness to act. Authentic accountability involves naming concerns early, clearly and respectfully before they become entrenched or personalised.

At the same time, accountability without fear recognises context. Leaders who take the time to understand workload, capacity and competing pressures are better placed to respond proportionately. Holding people to account does not mean ignoring the conditions in which they are working. It means balancing high expectations with realistic support, and challenge with curiosity. The question becomes not only 'what is not working?' but 'what is getting in the way?'

This balance is particularly important when leaders themselves are under pressure. In moments of stress, it is tempting to tighten control, increase monitoring or rely heavily on compliance mechanisms. These responses can feel reassuring in the short term; they create a sense of action and control, but they often signal a lack of trust and can unintentionally undermine professional autonomy. Authentic leaders resist the urge to manage anxiety by managing people more tightly.

Instead, they focus on consistency. Fairness in leadership is not about treating everyone the same; it is about applying principles reliably. When staff understand how decisions are made, how concerns are addressed and what leaders will and will not compromise on, trust grows even when decisions are difficult or unpopular. Consistency creates predictability, and predictability builds safety.

There will be times when accountability requires firmness. Authentic leadership does not shy away from this. There are moments when standards must be upheld clearly, when boundaries must be reinforced, and when inaction would signal a lack of care. The difference lies not in whether leaders act, but in how they do so with transparency, respect and an unwavering focus on purpose.

Leaders who hold the line without breaking people communicate belief as well as expectation. They make it clear that accountability exists because the work matters, because children deserve the best and because improvement is both possible and expected. This framing shifts accountability from something done *to* people to something carried *with* them.

Over time, cultures shaped by accountability without fear become stronger rather than weaker. People are more willing to take responsibility, to admit mistakes and to ask for help. Conversations become more honest. Standards are upheld not through surveillance or threat, but through shared commitment and professional pride.

Authentic leadership understands that accountability and trust are not opposites. They are interdependent. When leaders combine clarity with care, firmness with fairness and expectation with empathy, they create environments where people are held to account and held in mind (West, 2021).

Leading teams when the pressure is on

Staying steady when others are watching

Pressure changes everything.

Even the strongest teams feel different when the stakes rise. External scrutiny, time pressure, high-profile incidents, inspections or sudden crises can quickly shift dynamics. Conversations become shorter. Tolerance thins. People look upwards for certainty and reassurance. In these moments, leadership is not just about what is decided, but how leaders show up for others.

Authentic leadership under pressure is less about having the perfect response and more about providing steadiness. Teams do not need leaders who perform calmly while privately unravelling; they need leaders who are grounded enough to hold uncertainty without amplifying it. This does not mean pretending everything is fine. It means being emotionally regulated, clear in communication and consistent in behaviour.

When pressure mounts, teams often look to leaders for cues. They notice tone, body language, availability and presence. A hurried comment, a visible frustration or a lack of follow-up can be magnified far beyond its original intent. Conversely, small acts of steadiness, a measured response, a clear explanation or a willingness to listen can have a disproportionate calming effect.

One of the first tests of leadership under pressure is communication. In challenging moments, leaders can feel torn between sharing too much and saying too little. Over-communication can overwhelm; under-communication breeds anxiety and rumour. Authentic leaders aim for clarity rather than completeness. They share what they can, when they can and are honest about what is not yet known. Saying 'I don't have all the answers yet, but this is what we know so far' is often far more reassuring than silence or speculation.

Pressure also exposes how teams are led day to day. In cultures where trust has been built over time, teams are more likely to pull together when things are hard. Where trust is fragile, pressure can intensify fault lines. Leaders who have invested in relationships, clarity and shared responsibility before a crisis are better positioned to lead through it.

Another challenge under pressure is the temptation to centralise control. When leaders feel exposed or accountable, the instinct can be to hold decisions tightly, reduce autonomy and increase oversight. While some coordination is necessary in acute situations, sustained over-control can signal mistrust and disempower those who are best placed to help. Authentic leaders know when to step in and when to step back.

Leading teams under pressure also requires emotional intelligence. People respond differently to stress. Some become quieter; others become more vocal. Some seek reassurance; others withdraw. Effective leaders pay attention to these patterns without pathologising them. They recognise that behaviour under pressure is often communication and they respond with curiosity rather than judgement.

This does not mean absorbing everyone's emotions or trying to keep everyone comfortable. It means acknowledging impact without becoming overwhelmed by it. A simple recognition, 'I can see this is hard', can go a long way. Equally, leaders may need to set boundaries, refocus conversations or bring teams back to priorities when anxiety begins to dominate.

One of the most powerful things leaders can offer teams under pressure is a sense of purpose. Reminding people why the work matters, who it serves and what remains within their control can steady even the most turbulent moments. Purpose does not remove difficulty, but it gives it context. It shifts the focus from fear to meaning.

There will also be moments when leaders must make themselves visible. Being present physically or symbolically signals commitment and shared responsibility. This might mean showing up to difficult meetings, checking in with colleagues who are carrying heavy loads, or staying engaged when it would be easier to retreat into email and paperwork. Visibility, in these moments, is not about performance; it is about solidarity.

At the same time, leaders must guard against becoming the sole emotional anchor for the team. When everything flows through one person, pressure accumulates unsustainably. Authentic leadership distributes leadership, inviting others to step forward, to lead conversations, to support colleagues and to take ownership where appropriate. This not only lightens the load but also strengthens the team's collective capacity.

Under pressure, mistakes will happen. Decisions may need revisiting. Tensions may surface. Authentic leaders respond to these moments with reflection rather than defensiveness. They are willing to say, 'That didn't land as intended', or 'We need to adjust our approach'. This openness builds credibility rather than undermining it.

Leading teams when the pressure is on is ultimately about trust, trust in people, trust in shared values and trust in the process of working through complexity together. It requires leaders to be steady rather than heroic, present rather than perfect and clear rather than controlling.

When leaders hold themselves in this way, teams are more likely to feel safe, focused and capable even when circumstances are far from ideal. This is not about removing pressure, but about ensuring it does not define or distort the way leadership is lived; that too is how authentic leadership is done.

Strategy that doesn't lose its soul

Holding vision and values in long-term decisions

Strategy is often spoken about as something separate from values. It is associated with plans, priorities, timelines and outcomes, the practical machinery of leadership. Values, meanwhile, are sometimes treated as the softer companion: important, but secondary. In reality, strategy is one of the most powerful expressions of what a school truly values.

Every strategic decision answers a moral question, whether leaders name it or not.

What we choose to prioritise, invest in, pause or stop sends a clear signal about what matters. Which initiatives receive time and resources. Which pressures are absorbed and which are passed on. Which voices are amplified and which are quietly sidelined. Strategy is not neutral. It shapes culture long before it delivers outcomes.

Authentic leadership insists that strategy and values are held together.

In schools, strategic thinking is often crowded by immediacy. Urgent issues demand attention. External expectations shift. New initiatives arrive with little warning. Leaders can find themselves reacting rather than leading, responding to the loudest pressure rather than the deepest need. Over time, this reactivity can erode coherence. Staff feel overwhelmed. Purpose becomes blurred. Good ideas compete for limited energy.

Strategy that does not lose its soul begins with clarity of mission. Leaders need to be able to articulate, repeatedly and simply, what the school exists to do, who it is for and what it will not compromise on. This clarity becomes a filter. Not every opportunity needs to be taken. Not every demand needs to be met immediately. Strategic leadership involves saying no as often as saying yes.

This can be uncomfortable. Saying no can feel risky, particularly in systems that reward visible activity and constant improvement. Yet constant movement is not the same as meaningful progress. Authentic leaders resist the pressure to add endlessly, recognising that focus is a form of care. Protecting staff from overload is not a lack of ambition; it is a prerequisite for sustainability.

Values-led strategy also requires patience. Many of the most important changes in schools, cultural shifts, improvements in trust and deeper learning, unfold slowly. They do not always align neatly with inspection cycles or performance measures. Leaders committed to authenticity must hold their nerve, staying anchored to long-term purpose even when short-term validation is uncertain.

This does not mean ignoring data or accountability. It means interpreting them wisely. Data should inform judgement, not replace it. Numbers can highlight patterns and prompt questions, but they do not capture the full story of a school. Authentic leaders look beyond headline measures, asking what sits underneath, what is improving and what might be at risk of being lost in the pursuit of quick wins.

This alignment matters because strategy is enacted through people, not documents. When staff feel that strategic decisions honour their professionalism and reflect shared values, they are more likely to engage deeply. When strategy feels imposed or incoherent, compliance may follow, but commitment rarely does.

There is also a relational dimension to strategy that is often overlooked. Strategic decisions affect workload, identity and professional confidence. Leaders who acknowledge this and create space for dialogue, questions and challenge strengthen trust. They model that strategy is not something done to people, but something shaped with them.

Authentic leaders also recognise when strategy needs to be revisited. Holding values does not mean being inflexible. Contexts change. What was right at one moment may need adjusting at another. The key question is not 'have we stuck to the plan?' but 'are we still serving our purpose?' This requires humility as well as courage.

Perhaps most importantly, a strategy that retains its soul keeps people visible. In high-pressure environments, it is easy for human considerations to become secondary to systems and structures. Authentic leadership resists this drift. It keeps children, families and staff at the centre of strategic thinking – not as abstract beneficiaries, but as real people affected by every decision.

When leaders hold strategy and values together, they create coherence. Staff understand not just what is happening, but why. Decisions feel principled rather than reactive. Even when the path is demanding, there is a sense of direction and integrity.

Strategy, then, is not the opposite of authenticity. It is one of its most important expressions. When leaders allow strategy to be shaped by values and values to be tested through strategy, they build schools that are purposeful, resilient and deeply human.

That is how authentic leadership sustains itself over time.

Autonomy, trust and letting go

Growing others without disappearing

One of the quiet tensions in leadership is learning how to let go without losing sight of what matters. As leaders grow in responsibility, the instinct to hold things close can strengthen rather than fade. Decisions carry greater consequences. Accountability feels heavier. And when pressure is high, control can begin to feel like safety.

Yet sustainable leadership depends on the opposite.

Authentic leadership recognises that trust and autonomy are not optional extras; they are essential conditions for growth. Schools do not thrive when leadership is concentrated in a single role or a small group of people. They thrive when responsibility is shared, expertise is trusted and others are supported to lead in ways that are authentic to them.

Many leaders worry that granting autonomy means losing consistency, lowering standards or exposing the organisation to risk. These fears are understandable, particularly in systems that emphasise accountability and external judgement. But autonomy without clarity is chaos; autonomy with clarity is capacity-building. Authentic leaders are clear about purpose, expectations and boundaries and then create space for others to exercise judgement within them.

This balance matters because autonomy is deeply connected to trust. When leaders consistently step in, override decisions or rework others' contributions, the message received is rarely the one intended. What is heard is, 'I don't trust you', even when the leader's intention is support or protection. Over time, this erodes confidence and discourages initiative.

Trust, by contrast, invites ownership. When people feel trusted, they are more likely to take responsibility, to problem-solve and to invest emotionally in their work. They are also more likely to stay. In a profession grappling with recruitment and retention, autonomy is not a luxury; it is a strategy for sustainability (Education Support, 2022; NFER, 2023).

Authentic leaders understand that letting go often requires sitting with discomfort. Others will make decisions differently. Approaches may diverge. Mistakes will happen. The temptation to step back in, to correct, refine or take over can be strong. But growth rarely happens in perfectly controlled conditions. Leaders who allow space for learning signal confidence not only in others, but in themselves.

This does not mean leaders disappear. Autonomy does not remove accountability, and trust does not eliminate oversight. Authentic leadership involves staying connected without micromanaging, checking in rather than checking up. It involves asking questions that prompt reflection rather than issuing directives that close it down.

There is also a relational dimension to letting go. Leaders who hold on too tightly often do so out of care. They want to protect others from risk, criticism or failure. Yet protection can become limiting. When leaders consistently step in to rescue, they inadvertently communicate a lack of belief in others' capability. Letting go, when done thoughtfully, is a vote of confidence.

This is particularly important when developing future leaders. Aspiring leaders need opportunities to practise judgement, to navigate complexity and to experience the weight of decision-making with support, not substitution. Authentic leaders mentor, coach and guide, but they resist the urge to control outcomes. They allow others to find their own leadership voice.

Letting go also requires leaders to be honest about identity. For some, being needed has become part of how leadership is understood. Stepping back can feel like a loss of relevance or influence. Authentic leadership invites a different measure of impact, one that values what continues in your absence as much as what happens under your direct control.

Trust-based leadership creates resilience. When responsibility is distributed, organisations are less vulnerable to burnout, absence or change. Knowledge is shared rather than hoarded. Decisions are informed by those closest to the work. Leaders are freed to think strategically rather than constantly firefighting.

Of course, trust must be built. It grows through consistency, follow-through and integrity. Leaders cannot expect autonomy to flourish in environments where expectations are unclear or consequences feel unpredictable. Authentic leaders invest time in building the foundations of shared values, clear principles and strong relationships that make autonomy possible.

Letting go, then, is not a single act, but an ongoing practice. It requires leaders to continually ask themselves: *What do I need to hold, and what can I release? Where does my involvement add value and where might it limit growth?* These are not static answers; they evolve with context, people and experience.

When leaders trust others to lead, they do more than lighten their own load. They create schools where leadership is collective, confidence is grown and people feel valued not just for what they deliver, but for who they are becoming.

That is how authentic leadership multiplies itself.

Staying mission-focused when the noise is loud

Protecting purpose in a pressurised system

One of the greatest challenges for leaders today is not a lack of commitment or care, but the sheer volume of noise that surrounds the work. Policy changes, accountability measures, inspection frameworks, public commentary, media narratives and shifting priorities all compete for attention. In this environment, leaders can find themselves pulled in multiple directions at once, responding to what is loud rather than what is important.

Authentic leadership requires the discipline to filter noise without ignoring reality.

Schools do not operate in isolation. Leaders must engage with external expectations, statutory requirements and system-wide change. But not every demand deserves equal weight. The risk is not that leaders respond to pressure, but that they lose sight of purpose in the process. When everything feels urgent, purpose becomes diluted.

Staying mission-focused begins with clarity about why the school exists and who it serves. This clarity acts as an anchor. It allows leaders to evaluate new initiatives, directives and expectations against a core question: *Does this move us closer to our purpose, or does it distract us from it?* Without this filter, leaders can become reactive, constantly adjusting course without ever moving forward with intention.

Noise also shapes emotion. Constant scrutiny can create anxiety, defensiveness and a sense of being perpetually judged. Leaders may feel compelled to justify decisions rather than explain them, to perform confidence rather than practise it. Over time, this emotional strain can erode authenticity, as leaders begin to lead for approval rather than alignment (Schein, 2010).

Authentic leaders resist this drift by grounding themselves in values rather than validation. They are clear about what success looks like on their own terms, not just in external metrics. This does not mean rejecting accountability, but it does mean holding it in proportion. Inspection outcomes, performance data and public narratives matter, but they are not the whole story.

Another challenge of noise is how it filters into schools. When leaders absorb pressure without processing it, it often passes directly to staff. Urgency multiplies.

Workload intensifies. Anxiety spreads. Authentic leadership involves acting as a buffer as well as a conduit, translating external demands into manageable, meaningful action rather than amplifying stress.

This buffering role requires judgement. Leaders must decide what to pass on, what to pause and what to push back on. Not everything that arrives needs immediate action. Sometimes the most responsible response is to wait, to seek clarity or to decide that an initiative will not be pursued. Saying no, or not yet, is a leadership act.

Mission-focused leadership also requires courage. There will be times when leaders must hold a steady course in the face of criticism or scepticism. Values-led decisions may not always align neatly with prevailing narratives. In these moments, authenticity is tested. Leaders must ask themselves whether they are willing to stand by their principles when doing so carries risk.

This is particularly true in systems that reward compliance and visibility. Authentic leaders understand that not all good work is immediately seen or celebrated. Some of the most important leadership actions, building trust, developing staff and supporting vulnerable pupils, unfold quietly over time. Staying mission-focused means valuing this work even when it is not easily measured.

Leaders also need spaces to think. Noise fills any vacuum left by reflection. Authentic leadership involves creating time for sense-making individually and collectively. This might mean stepping back to review priorities, revisiting values with leadership teams or simply pausing before responding to the latest demand. Thoughtful leadership is not slow leadership; it is deliberate leadership.

Another aspect of staying mission-focused is protecting hope. Constant exposure to pressure and criticism can lead to cynicism, where leaders and staff alike begin to question whether their efforts make a difference. Authentic leaders counter this by naming progress, celebrating growth and reminding their communities of the impact of their work. Hope, in this sense, is not naïve optimism; it is a strategic resource.

Ultimately, staying mission-focused when the noise is loud is about choosing where to place attention and energy. Leaders cannot control every external influence, but they can control what they amplify within their organisation. They can choose to centre purpose over panic, values over volume and meaning over momentum.

When leaders do this consistently, they create schools that feel grounded rather than reactive. Staff understand what matters and why. Decisions feel principled rather than performative. Even in turbulent systems, there is a sense of direction and integrity.

That is how authentic leadership protects purpose and why it matters now more than ever.

What this looks like on an ordinary day

Living authentic leadership in the small moments

Authentic leadership is rarely forged in the dramatic moments people talk about later. It does not live primarily in crisis meetings, inspection outcomes or public recognition. More often, it is shaped and revealed in the ordinary days, the routines, conversations and small decisions that quietly accumulate into culture.

On an ordinary day, authentic leadership might look like taking a moment before responding to an email that triggers frustration, choosing clarity over reactivity. It might be stopping in a corridor to really listen, even when time is tight. It might be acknowledging uncertainty rather than masking it, or saying 'I need to think about that' instead of offering an immediate answer.

These moments rarely feel significant at the time. Yet they are noticed.

Staff watch how leaders speak about pupils when they are not present. They notice how disagreement is handled in meetings, whether a challenge is welcomed or closed down. They pay attention to whose voices are amplified, whose concerns are acted on and whose are quietly dismissed. Over time, these signals shape what people believe is safe, valued and possible.

On ordinary days, authentic leadership shows up in consistency. Doing what you said you would do. Returning to agreed principles when decisions are difficult. Holding boundaries kindly but firmly. Consistency builds trust, not because leaders are perfect, but because they are predictable in their values.

It also shows up in how leaders manage their own presence. Leaders who are constantly rushed, unavailable or visibly overwhelmed unintentionally communicate urgency and scarcity. Leaders who model calm focus, even amid pressure, create space for others to think and act more deliberately. This is not about personality; it is about self-awareness.

Authentic leadership on ordinary days also involves noticing what is being carried and by whom. It means paying attention to workload, emotional strain and the cumulative impact of decisions. Sometimes this leads to action; sometimes it simply leads to acknowledgement. Both matter. Feeling seen is often a prerequisite for feeling trusted.

There are ordinary moments, too, when leaders choose courage over comfort. Naming an issue that others are avoiding. Challenging a narrative that feels misaligned with values. Protecting a colleague or a child when doing so is inconvenient. These moments are rarely applauded, but they shape the moral climate of a school.

Just as importantly, authentic leadership includes moments of restraint. Not stepping in immediately. Allowing others to lead. Letting a process unfold rather than controlling it. Trust is often built not through action, but through deliberate non-intervention.

On ordinary days, leaders also make choices about what to attend to. What is celebrated. What is overlooked. What becomes urgent, and what is allowed time. These choices signal priorities more powerfully than any strategic document. Over time, they teach people what really matters.

Authentic leadership is therefore not something leaders switch on for important occasions. It is a way of being that shows up repeatedly, quietly and imperfectly. It involves making the best decisions you can, reflecting when things do not land as intended, and adjusting with humility rather than defensiveness.

Perhaps most reassuringly, authentic leadership on ordinary days allows leaders to be human. To learn. To get things wrong and put them right. To grow alongside the people they lead. This humanity does not weaken authority; it strengthens credibility.

When leaders attend to these small moments with intention, they create schools where trust feels real, purpose feels shared and leadership feels grounded rather than performative. Nothing dramatic may happen on any given day, but over time, everything changes.

That is how authentic leadership is lived. Not all at once. But every day.

Reflection: Leadership in practice

Take a moment to pause

This chapter has focused on the everyday practices of leadership, the routines, decisions and interactions that quietly shape culture over time. These reflections invite you to look beneath what is done, and consider *how* it is done, *why* and *with what impact*. They are not about perfection, but about intentionality.

Reflect on leadership practice

- Which daily leadership routines in your role carry the most influence, even if they feel small or unnoticed?
- How consistently do your actions reflect the values you say matter most?
- Where might habit be driving behaviour more than conscious choice?

Practice is where leadership becomes visible.

Reflect on consistency and credibility

- Are there moments where what you say and what you do risk drifting apart?
- How do you respond when practice is challenged by time pressure or competing priorities?
- What do others experience as 'typical' of your leadership on a difficult day?

Credibility is built in patterns, not promises.

Reflect on people and relationships

- Who do you check in with regularly, and who might be missing from that picture?
- How do you show appreciation for effort that is quiet, relational or unseen?
- When mistakes occur, what message does your response send about trust and learning?

Leadership is experienced through relationships before it is understood through strategy.

Reflect on courage in practice

- When was the last time you adjusted your practice because it didn't align with your values?
- Where might avoiding discomfort be limiting the impact of your leadership?
- How confident are you that others feel safe to question 'how things are done' in your setting?

Authentic leadership is sustained through courage in the everyday.

Look ahead

- What one leadership practice could you refine this term to better reflect your values?
- Where might greater clarity or consistency make a meaningful difference to others?
- How will you ensure that *how* things are done remains as important as *what* is done?

References

Education Support. (2022). *Teacher Wellbeing Index 2022*. Education Support.

Fullan, M. (2014). *The Principal: Three Keys to Maximising Impact*. Jossey-Bass.

Heifetz, R., Grashow, A., & Linsky, M (2009). *The Practice of Adaptive Leadership: Tools and Tactics for Changing Your Organization and the World*. Harvard Business Press.

National Foundation for Educational Research (NFER). (2023). *Teacher Labour Market in England Annual Report 2023*. NFER.

Schein, E. (2010). *Organizational Culture and Leadership* (4th ed.). Jossey-Bass.

West, M. (2021). *Compassionate Leadership: Sustaining Wisdom, Humanity and Presence in Health and Social Care*. Swirling Leaf Press.

10 Wearing the badge

The Headteacher badge

Now this Leadership badge has the potential to take on a whole different level of behaviours if you let it. I chose to remember the behaviours of leaders I had interacted with in the past, and I encourage you to, also remember the behaviours of leaders you've interacted with in the past and include them in your 'how not to lead' leadership toolkit, because if you can do that, your ability to lead with authenticity will forever be your DNA.

You're being read all the time

Just like as a Deputy, you are on show 24/7, and if you inherit a school with staff who would rather an alternative candidate was chosen, you know you are being watched like a hawk! For the second time in my career, I am successful over the internal candidate and find myself grappling with how to manage the relationship. It's not an easy situation for anyone to find themselves in, so having a deep level of empathy felt like the only way to manage the situation. Sensitive interactions, often being more accommodating than maybe I should have been, but at the time, it felt the right thing to do.

For the purpose of this section on the Headteacher badge, finding the Headship, which you can call 'home', a place where you can thrive, make a difference, leading young people and adults, has got to be the most wonderful, humbling, inspiring opportunity ever. When I became a Headteacher in a school that had just received an Ofsted Requires Improvement judgement, I was determined to work with staff to improve outcomes and standards and to do so rapidly. The young people could not wait. Sometimes in our hurry to make improvements, we can forget that every person in the organisation makes up part of the puzzle, and so knowing what they bring, their strengths and areas for improvement is important. I had the privilege of time to be able to meet nearly all members of staff before I joined and to 'get under

DOI: 10.4324/9781003635666-10

the skin' as to what the challenges were in the school. Fore-armed is fore-warned, and as a leader that is immensely helpful.

Becoming a Headteacher is very different to being a Deputy Headteacher in terms of responsibilities; the buck really does stop with you, but I think good Leadership is about recognising what you're good at and the areas that others are much better at than you. That, for me, was authenticity, resisting the pressure to project certainty and choosing honesty about what I did and did not know yet. So I took this mindset into my Headship, drawing upon my strong skill set of building positive relationships and teams, knowing when and how to have those difficult but necessary conversations and finding the 'gems' in everyone. I truly believe that those who go into education do so with a passion and a drive to want to make a difference, to contribute something quite powerful, but sometimes, they forget their purpose, can become cynical and lose their way. The skill of a good leader is to find it, to reignite it so they can be the best version of themselves. I think I was able to do this in a way that meant that even when those necessary conversations were had, they were carried out with dignity and respect so that colleagues could still leave my office, head held high.

The tension between image and integrity

There is something here, therefore, about that tension between image and integrity in leadership. Rhett Power, in his Forbes article, 'Why Authentic Leaders Win Influence and Trust at Work', summarises what I strived to achieve during my time as a Senior Leader. He reminds us that we are 'living in an era where leaders are expected to be transparent, genuine, relatable and values-driven. Being skilled or strategic isn't the only priority'. As leaders in schools, trusts and colleges, this is so relatable as we are thrust into the limelight to comment on policy changes, political musings, community concerns, as well as navigate complex political neutrality rules, even when discussing topics like climate change, racism or gender identity, often with little support or clarity.

Power asks us to consider how we strike the right balance so that when authenticity is practised well, we are able to build trust and influence because when misapplied, it creates confusion, instability and even fear. This takes me back to my earlier point of building relationships, getting to know your staff, investing time to know at least one thing about every member of staff, no matter how small and why, because it shows that you care.

When coaching new Headteachers, they often ask me about this balance, how can you be open without oversharing, how can you maintain that professional line so that you've shared just enough to seem human but can still have authority. A quick response I learnt early on in Headship is that your staff are not your friends, you probably have enough, and so do they! It's not uncommon for staff to meet for drinks at the end of term, and whilst you may be invited, the trick is to go, have one drink, buy a round of drinks and then leave. Staff will see that you're human, you wanted to spend social time with them, but you respect their space to let their hair down, as it were.

Clarify your intent, not just your feelings

We often equate authenticity with speaking off the cuff or 'telling it like it is'. But that's not authenticity, it's really impulsivity. The most trusted leaders are real and intentional. They say what they feel in the moment and take time to share the why behind the what. That's what creates clarity, and clarity builds trust.

Real and intentional are two areas that I think some leaders may struggle with; I know I did in the early days of headship. What's real to me is that I grew up in North West London, times were hard and leaving school with no qualifications meant that as a leader I would often (and still do) find myself in spaces where I feel vulnerable. So do I keep it real when the topic for discussion is something I know very little about, like Plato or Aristotle, or do I pretend I know more than I do? Over time and as my confidence has grown, in those types of situations, I've learnt to keep it real, and I'll be open and ask questions rather than offer a reflection. But his point about clarifying your intent is something I can get behind. When launching a new initiative, policy or practice, staff just want to know 'why are we doing this'. Behaviour is a concern; we have an increase in truancy, so what is going to happen is that the senior team will increase their corridor walks, and Heads of Years will be added to the rota to add capacity. This explains the why behind the what will be happening and creates clarity, which most staff will be able to support.

Strike a balance between transparency and restraint

This is the tightrope walk of leadership authenticity. Overshare, and you might sound selfish or unstable. Under-share, and you might leave your team uncertain and guessing, and we all know that when staff are left to guess they often assume the worst.

There is also something here about emotional transparency. I have worked in schools where staff find it hard to keep their emotions in check. There is a school of thought that in being authentic, leaders should be able to cry if they feel the need, share that something is making them feel sad, angry, disappointed, etc., but my view, similar to Powers, is that there has to be the right balance. After all, when leaders try to be 'raw and real' by expressing every emotion they feel in the momen, it doesn't create a connection; it creates chaos. Conversely, 'leaders who stay silent during pivotal moments. That silence doesn't communicate strength, but rather it creates a vacuum, and vacuums get filled with fear'. An Ofsted inspection is a good example of the need for leaders to demonstrate this level of balance. We all know what it means and feels like 'to get the call'. Your heart sinks, your stomach does summersaults, and you're already thinking what personal diary commitments you are going to have to cancel, childcare arrangements you will have to make and the disappointment you will have to endure from the people you had planned to see but will now not see for at least three days! You carry all of this as you bring your Teams together, stand in the assembly hall and share the news with your staff, but does it show no. You can voice, 'Ofsted inspections are never easy', but you lean into the trust and relationships you've built and assure everyone, 'we've got this'. The point here is to share enough to offer clarity and show humanity, but not so much that we overwhelm or confuse everyone. The words Ofsted and Easy probably feel a juxtaposition of words here, but I hope you get the sentiment of what transparency vs restraint in the school context means here.

> Authenticity isn't a free pass to say whatever you want. It's a discipline and a leadership skill. And in a world where trust is fragile and attention spans are short, leaders who practice authentic communication, not just authentic emotion, stand out.
>
> (Rhett Power, 2025)

The weight of the badge

The badge amplifies everything

Becoming a Headteacher changes how you are seen. Whether you want it to or not, the badge amplifies you. Your words carry further. Your silences are noticed. Your reactions are read for meaning.

That can be unsettling, particularly for leaders who value humility, collaboration and warmth. But wearing the badge does not require you to become someone else. It asks you to become more intentional about who you already are.

The mistake many new headteachers make is believing they must perform the role rather than inhabit it. They feel pressure to appear confident at all times, decisive in every moment, and emotionally neutral regardless of what they are carrying. Over time, that performance becomes exhausting and inauthentic.

Authentic leadership does not mean discarding the badge, nor hiding behind it. It means understanding the power it brings and choosing how to use it wisely.

The badge will test your integrity. It will place you in situations where being liked and being respected pull in different directions. It will invite you to overshare at times, and to retreat into silence at others. The discipline of authentic leadership is knowing when to speak, when to listen and when to hold the line quietly.

Worn well, the badge does not distance you from your people. It reassures them. It signals steadiness, clarity and care. It reminds others and yourself that leadership is not about performance, but presence.

The badge does not make you a leader. But it does reveal the kind of leader you are becoming.

Leadership reflection: Wearing the badge

Take a moment to pause

Stepping into headship brings visibility, authority and expectation. The badge is symbolic, but the responsibility it represents is real. This reflection invites you to consider how identity, communication and authenticity show up once you are seen as *the* leader.

Reflect on stepping into the role

- How did it feel when you first received the Headteacher badge?
- What planning did you or might you do before starting the role?
- What assumptions did others make about you once you were wearing the badge?

Leadership identity often shifts before leaders have time to process it.

Reflect on experience and learning

- What lessons did you learn in Deputy Headteacher roles that now shape how you lead?
- Which experiences prepared you most for the moral weight of headship?
- Where did you learn what *not* to carry forward?

Experience informs authenticity as much as aspiration.

Reflect on communication and discipline

- Has there been a time when you practised authentic communication rather than authentic emotion? What impact did that have?
- How do you decide what to share, when to share it and how?
- Where does emotional regulation become a leadership responsibility rather than a personal choice?

Authenticity is not a free pass to say whatever we feel. It is a discipline and a leadership skill.

Look ahead

- How will you continue to practise authenticity with intention as visibility increases?

- What commitments will you make to communicate with clarity, care and purpose?
- In a context where trust is fragile and attention spans are short, how will you ensure your words strengthen confidence rather than erode it?

Reference

Power, R. (2025). Why authentic leaders win influence and trust at work. *Forbes*.

11 The challenges

Leading when leadership isn't easy

If there is one universal truth in school leadership, it is this: no one escapes the challenges. Not the new leader finding their feet, not the seasoned head who has 'seen it all' and certainly not those of us who walk into a school where the culture feels bruised, the trust is thin and the expectations are sky-high. Challenges are not the exception; they are the rhythm of leadership. And yet, how we respond to them is what separates leaders who merely survive from those who lead with authenticity, purpose and grace.

Research across education and public-sector leadership increasingly points to a shift in the nature of challenge itself (Education Support, 2022; NFER, 2023). Leaders are operating in environments characterised by heightened accountability, public scrutiny, workforce instability and overlapping social pressures. Studies exploring leadership stress and moral load suggest that what makes contemporary challenges feel more demanding is not volume alone, but complexity: leaders are required to make decisions that carry ethical, relational and emotional consequences simultaneously. Evidence indicates that when leaders hold responsibility for performance alongside wellbeing, safeguarding, inclusion and retention, the challenge becomes cumulative rather than episodic. This helps explain why even experienced leaders report fatigue, doubt and a sense that challenges linger longer than they once did. The difficulty, therefore, is not a lack of resilience, but the sustained weight of responsibility carried in systems with limited margin for error.

When I look back over my own career, I realise that the challenges didn't just shape me, they revealed me. They exposed what I really believed about people, about children, about justice, about fairness and about myself. Challenges have a way of holding up a mirror. Sometimes you like what you see; sometimes you don't. But if you're brave enough, each challenge becomes an invitation: *Are you still going to lead as you? Or are you going to shrink, contort, adjust, perform?*

Authentic leadership is not tested when everything is going well. Anyone can 'lead' when results look rosy, behaviour is calm, budgets balance and you have a stable senior team. Authentic leadership is tested when you're standing in the

DOI: 10.4324/9781003635666-11

middle of the storm, when you're dealing with a safeguarding incident that keeps you awake at night, when you're holding a colleague through their professional crisis, when the press decided your school is their latest headline, or when you walk into a classroom and see something you simply cannot ignore.

The challenge *the real challenge* is remaining yourself through all of this.

In the education sector, we talk a lot about resilience, grit, strategy and accountability. But less often do we name the quieter challenges: the loneliness of leadership; the emotional labour; the constant negotiation between being compassionate and being decisive; the feeling that everyone wants a piece of you. And for some of us, additional layers are being the only Black woman in a leadership space, or the only leader of colour, the only one who sounds 'different', looks 'different' or thinks differently. The challenge there is not only to succeed, but to succeed without losing yourself.

Three categories of challenge

Over the years, I have learnt that challenges come in three broad categories:

1. **The challenges of the system**: Funding, inspection frameworks, recruitment crises, political rhetoric and shifting expectations.
2. **The challenges of the school**: Culture, behaviour, morale, safeguarding, curriculum and parental pressures.
3. **The challenges within ourselves**: Doubt, imposter syndrome, burnout, the urge to please everyone and the temptation to perform instead of lead.

And it is often the third category, the internal challenges that leaders rarely talk about openly. Yet these are the challenges that most threaten our authenticity. These are the moments when the temptation to 'code-switch' is at its greatest, when we wonder whether being ourselves will be enough or whether we need to adopt someone else's leadership persona to be taken seriously.

But here's the truth I learnt the hard way:

When the challenges come, and they will, leading as someone else will not save you. Leading as yourself will.

The purpose of this chapter is not to depress you, but to prepare you. To name the challenges with honesty, but also with hope. To show you that the messy, complex, deeply human challenges are not evidence you're failing, they're evidence you're leading.

And more importantly:

You can face every single challenge without abandoning who you are.

Along the way, there have been a few hard-won lessons that I wish someone had told me earlier in my career. Because whilst challenges are unavoidable, losing yourself in them is not. Authentic leadership is not the easy route. But it is the only sustainable one.

The system challenges: Leading in a landscape that moves faster than you do

One of the earliest realisations you have as a leader is that you are not just leading a school, you are leading within a system that is constantly shifting. Sometimes gently, sometimes violently. And you are expected to remain steady through all of it.

I remember one particular period during my headship when the *guidance* changed so frequently that we barely had time to embed one set of expectations before a new set landed in our inboxes. At the height of the pandemic, Department for Education (DfE) updates were dropping at 5 pm on a Friday or at the start of a holiday, with leaders scrambling to interpret, implement and communicate changes overnight. And even after the pandemic, the volume of shifting guidance on attendance, curriculum expectations, assessment, exclusions, uniform, safeguarding and behavioural standards felt relentless. Each update nudged the goalposts just enough to unsettle the ground beneath us, and yet, as leaders, we were still expected to carry the weight calmly, reassure staff confidently and communicate to parents convincingly. Leadership in schools isn't just about vision; it is about navigating an unpredictable landscape with grace.

According to the National Foundation for Educational Research (NFER), rapid policy change is now one of the top three drivers of leader stress, with leaders reporting that the pace of change often outstrips their capacity to plan and embed meaningful improvement. Leaders don't fear change; they fear incoherent change. They fear change with no runway, no narrative, no support behind it.

And yet, amid the turbulence, leaders still show up. They still lead with purpose.

But the challenge here is this: *How do you remain authentic when the system itself feels uncertain?*

For some, the temptation is to retreat into compliance mode, tick every box, say yes to everything and try desperately to stay 'safe'. But authenticity in these moments requires a different kind of bravery: the bravery to hold your nerve, to advocate for what you know is right for your pupils and to model calm leadership even when you are quietly firefighting behind closed doors.

I often say to leaders: 'The system will always shift. Your authenticity is the one stabilising force that cannot'.

The school challenges: The human complexity behind the headlines

Schools are living, breathing ecosystems. They are not spreadsheets; they are not neat. They are messy, emotional, unpredictable places full of people with hopes, fears, trauma, gifts, needs and opinions. Every corridor, every classroom, every office holds a story. Leadership, therefore, is fundamentally relational.

When I became Headteacher of a school that had just been judged requires improvement, I walked straight into a culture that was tired, defensive and uncertain. The previous inspection had deeply bruised people. Staff were fearful. Some were angry. Others were simply exhausted. You can't 'strategy' your way out of that. You have to be present with people. You have to listen. You have to sit in the discomfort and understand the emotional landscape you've inherited.

And you have to do this while still being the one everyone looks to for answers.

The Education Support's Teacher Wellbeing Index (2023) reports that *school culture and leadership style are the strongest predictors of whether staff stay or leave*, more so than pay or workload. In other words:

People don't leave schools; they leave climates. They leave how they feel in that climate.

This is why the school-based challenges cut the deepest:

- A colleague who is struggling but too proud to say.
- A middle leader who feels overwhelmed but keeps smiling.
- A difficult parental complaint that shakes a teacher's confidence.
- A behaviour crisis that tests the culture you've worked so hard to build.
- A safeguarding concern that lives with you long after the building is locked.

These challenges don't simply test your competence; they test your capacity for compassion, your ability to hold boundaries and your willingness to stay anchored to your values even when the emotional temperature rises.

And again, the challenge is subtle but profound:

How do you remain human in an environment that sometimes demands superhuman resilience?

Authenticity here means allowing yourself to feel the weight of responsibility without letting it crush you. It means having difficult conversations with dignity. It means modelling calm, even when inside you are dancing between ten competing priorities. It means being honest enough to say, 'This is hard', but strong enough to say, 'And we will find a way through'.

The inner challenges: The ones no one sees but every leader feels

If leaders truly wrote down what keeps them awake at night, the list would be far longer than any job description.

There are the obvious ones: *safeguarding, staffing, Ofsted, budgets, behaviour, attendance.*

But the deepest challenges are often the ones hidden in plain sight:

- *Am I good enough?*
- *Am I making the right decision?*
- *Do people trust me?*
- *What if I let everyone down?*
- *What if today I'm not as strong as they need me to be?*

For leaders from underrepresented backgrounds, there are added layers:

- *Will I be judged more harshly?*
- *Do I need to sound a certain way to be taken seriously?*
- *Is being myself enough?*

A wide body of research in organisational psychology, including Clance and Imes' foundational 1978 study, McKinsey's 'Onlyness' data and more recent analyses by Bravata et al., shows that imposter feelings disproportionately affect women and global majority leaders (Clance & Imes, 1978; Bravata et al., 2020; McKinsey, 2021). This isn't due to ability, but to navigating environments where they are under-represented, over-scrutinised or expected to code-switch to 'fit'. These dynamics create fertile ground for self-doubt, even among the most capable leaders.

This is a challenge few talk about openly, yet it shapes leadership profoundly.

I remember when I first became a Deputy Head. I would walk into a room full of senior leaders and instantly feel the need to 'sound more senior', whatever that meant. It took time and courage to unlearn that. To realise that authenticity was not a risk; it was my strength. It was the thing that would hold me together when the challenges came.

And here is the truth most leaders eventually discover:

The hardest person you will ever have to lead is yourself.

Your thoughts. Your doubts. Your emotions. Your expectations.

Your 'what ifs'. Your 'should haves'. Your 'why didn't I think of that sooner?'

Authentic leadership isn't just a leadership style; it is a daily decision to show up as yourself, even when your self feels tired, stretched or uncertain.

These inner challenges matter because they shape how we face all the others. A leader who knows themselves, truly knows themselves, is far harder to knock off balance.

When every decision feels high-stakes: The weight of being 'the one'

One of the hidden challenges of leadership is that you quickly become the person everyone looks to for certainty, for calm, for solutions, for hope. Whether you feel ready or not. Whether you feel confident or not. Whether you feel like a leader or simply someone doing their best on very little sleep.

It took me years to understand that leadership carries an invisible weight: *the burden of other people's expectations.*

- Staff expect you to have the answers.
- Parents expect you to fix everything.
- Governors expect you to deliver the plan.
- Students expect you to protect them.
- The community expects you to hold the school together.
- And the system expects you to do all of this with a smile, a policy document and a spreadsheet.

What no-one tells you is that this weight doesn't just sit on your shoulders, it sits in your mind, your heart and, if you're not careful, your sense of self.

There is research to back this up, too. The Education Support *School Leaders' Wellbeing Report* (2023) shows that *74% of Headteachers report significant stress,* with the majority saying the pressure of decision-making is one of the biggest contributing factors. Leaders often fear 'getting it wrong' not because of ego, but because of the potential impact on staff or students.

Authentic leadership does not remove the weight, but it helps you carry it honestly.

You learn to replace perfection with clarity.

You learn to replace certainty with courage.

And you learn that sometimes the most authentic thing you can say is:

I don't have all the answers yet, but I will work with you to find them.

The challenge of leading in the public eye: When your leadership becomes a story

Another challenge that few people fully appreciate until they sit in the chair is this: leadership is increasingly public.

A single complaint can end up on social media.

A decision taken in good faith can be misinterpreted by those outside the room.

An internal matter can become external within hours, sometimes minutes.

One inaccurate comment can spread faster than the truth.

In the era of WhatsApp groups, online forums, community Facebook pages and viral posts, school leaders are often managing *perceptions* as much as reality.

During the pandemic, I remember the surreal feeling of reading comments about decisions we'd made, decisions rooted in safeguarding, wellbeing and public health, only to see them critiqued by people who hadn't read a single line of the guidance that was hitting our inboxes at 5 pm on a Friday. It would have been easy to take it personally, but I learned quickly that in leadership, visibility comes with vulnerability.

This isn't about trying to please everyone; that is impossible.

It's about standing by decisions that align with your values, even when the noise around you is loud.

Brené Brown talks about 'strong back, soft front', and this could not be more relevant for school leaders. A strong back: clarity, courage, values. A soft front: empathy, humility, humanity. The combination is what allows leaders to withstand criticism without becoming defensive, and to stay compassionate without becoming overwhelmed.

The authentic leader's challenge is this:

How do you remain human while being scrutinised?

The answer, I've learnt, is by letting your values, not the noise, guide the story you tell.

A leadership challenge in real time

Some leadership challenges are theoretical. Others arrive without warning, unfolding in real time, under public scrutiny and without the safety of hindsight.

What follows is a reflection from a serving headteacher, Manny Botwe, written in the aftermath of one such moment. It captures the reality of leading when symbols, identity, belonging and community tensions collide and when every possible decision carries risk.

This is not a neat case study with a clear resolution. It is a lived leadership dilemma. One that asks uncomfortable questions about voice, neutrality, silence and courage, particularly in contexts where leaders are expected to hold competing truths at once.

I include Manny's reflection here not because it offers easy answers, but because it reveals what authentic leadership looks like when certainty is unavailable, and the cost of action or inaction is deeply human.

Flags, belonging and the importance of using your voice – Manny Botwe, Headteacher, Tytherington School

The first time I became aware of St Georges' flags going up around the country was when I came into school on the penultimate Wednesday of August. Senior leaders will be aware that schools receive the results one day before the official publication, so I was nervously driving into school, wondering how the students had got on. As I got within 100 metres of my school, I saw a couple of St Georges' flags which had been put up on the street lamps. They looked a little unusual because of the homespun nature of how they had been put up. I assumed that someone had put them up following the success of the Lionesses a few weeks earlier and perhaps had forgotten to take them down. I didn't really think much more about it until the end of the day.

As I drove home, I happened to be on the phone with a local Head. He mentioned something called 'Operation Raise the Colours' – a campaign encouraging people to fly flags outside their homes. I nodded, made a mental note and thought no more about it. It felt like yet another passing internet phenomenon in a world already saturated with them.

But as the school year started and pupils returned, more flags began to appear around the town and in other local areas. Not just one or two, but clusters across whole neighbourhoods. Little by little, they shifted from background decoration to something that demanded interpretation.

Depending on who you asked, they were harmless expressions of pride or coded statements about who belonged and who didn't. This was something I was really uncomfortable about getting involved in. Firstly, the school community I serve is predominantly white British. I have to admit that I was scared about the response the local community might have if I came out and declared that I was unhappy or confused about this. Secondly, the fact that the government of the day appeared to be equivocating on how the flags were making people feel made me feel like I was out on a limb as a Headteacher.

The turning point came one evening when an email arrived from a parent of a mixed-heritage family. I had known the parent for several years, and he has three children at my school. It was not an angry email. It was not a political email. It was a letter written by a parent trying to make sense of what was happening on their own street. They described how exposed he personally felt when two St Georges' flags appeared on his street. He talked about how he felt when he took his sons to play a football match in another local town where the streets were filled with flags. Facebook posts and WhatsApp groups, which had previously felt like safe spaces with old school friends, had now turned into arenas of debates about immigration. Although he had been born and bred in Macclesfield, he was beginning to feel like an outsider.

It was the kind of letter school leaders receive from time to time, the quiet kind, sent late in the evening, containing more truth than the sender probably realised.

Leadership sometimes comes in the form of messages that say, without quite saying it, 'Please don't look away. We need to hear your voice on this one'.

By pure coincidence on that evening, as I went for a late-night walk around my village, I saw a gentleman putting up a flag on a street lamp. I did not know what to do. Should I confront them? Chances are that I would probably know them. What would I say? I made the decision to turn left and try to complete my late-night walk. These are the day-to-day decisions people of colour have to make every day.

Anyway, I decided that we needed to confront the issue head-on. If I, a Black Headteacher for 11 years and former Association of School and College Leaders President, could not come out and talk about how I was feeling, then what hope was there? Before doing anything publicly, I started with the staff. In briefings, corridor conversations and pastoral meetings, I asked how pupils were talking about the flags, other symbols and listened for the temperature in the building. Staff were picking up the same undercurrents: curiosity from some pupils, anxiety from others and for a small minority, an unsettling fascination with the performative side of flag culture. The message from staff was consistent: 'We need to do something before this becomes something'.

Part of what made the situation so difficult was the vacuum at the national level. Politicians across the spectrum declined to comment, anxious to avoid inflaming their own constituencies or being accused of 'taking sides'. Guidance from government was conspicuously absent. Public bodies kept silent. In another era, the kind of cultural tensions emerging in our streets would have prompted ministerial statements or at least a measured public framing. This time, there was nothing.

That silence had consequences. It meant that schools became the only civic institution that could not opt out. While others could remain neutral, school leaders found themselves alone at the fault line, without cover and without a steer. The flags had become a national conversation that nobody in national leadership was willing to have, so it became a conversation happening in corridors, classrooms and playgrounds instead. In the absence of national leadership, local leadership had to step up.

I decided to act in a sequence: parents first, then staff, then students, in that order. Families needed to know that we were approaching the issue through the lens of belonging, not partisan politics. In my weekly Headteacher's Notes, sent a week in advance of the assembly, I previewed the theme and set the tone. I wrote about symbols, stories and why comprehensive schools matter so deeply because they remain one of the few places where children from profoundly different backgrounds share space and identity. I wrote about the importance of empathy and how we can disagree without dissolving the ties that bind us together as a community.

Staff preparation mattered too. Assemblies that touch on identity and belonging cannot be done as 'theatrical one-offs'. I met with pastoral leaders beforehand to ensure tutor groups were ready for follow-up discussion and that any student disclosures about identity, family anxiety or experiences of exclusion could be handled safely and well. Staff appreciated that we were not springing it on them. One commented, 'Thank you for getting ahead of this; it's been bubbling'.

The assembly itself was titled *Symbols, Stories and Belonging*. I opened by asking what a symbol is and how context changes meaning. A flag on a ship means one thing. A flag on a house means another. A flag in a moment of celebration means something different from a flag in a moment of polarisation. We spoke about skin in the game, about the backstories we all carry, and about how multi-layered British identity really is. I shared my own family story, my parents arriving from Ghana, my wife's family from Lancashire farming stock, our children, Cheshire-born and how all of those threads are part of the tapestry of Britain today.

I talked about my own experience. I play five-a-side football with a group of lads every week. At Christmas, we go into the local town and have a few drinks and a meal based on money accrued from our weekly subs across the year. I had noticed that on the high street of the town we usually go out in, it was covered with St Georges' flags. Sadly, I felt that I needed to give the Christmas drinks a miss because I did not feel comfortable. I have not felt this way since the 1980s. This struck a chord with the youngsters.

We also explored why we sometimes fly the Union flag in school and what we are signalling when we do: this is our country. Everyone has a voice. Everyone belongs. We may disagree, but we are one community. These weren't slogans; they were values.

But assemblies alone don't change culture. The more important leadership work happened afterwards on lunch duty, at the school gate and in corridors.

Looking back, I learned that authentic leadership is less about having the perfect answer and more about creating conditions where students and staff can continue to belong to one another across differences. The quiet decisions matter: the letter that is answered compassionately; the briefing that steadies staff; the assembly that reframes the debate; the conversation on duty that signals, 'I see you'.

In a year where flags appeared everywhere, our task was not to pick one. Our task was to make sure every child knew that the only banner that mattered inside our gates was the one that read: everyone belongs.

Research into leadership wellbeing and retention highlights the cumulative cost of unresolved challenge, particularly in professions with high moral responsibility. Studies on moral distress suggest that leaders experience significant strain when they are repeatedly required to act in ways that conflict with their values, or when systemic constraints prevent them from doing what they believe is right (Education Support, 2022; NFER, 2023). Over time, this dissonance can lead to emotional exhaustion, withdrawal and a reduced sense of professional efficacy. Evidence from workforce wellbeing research indicates that leaders are more likely to disengage or leave roles not because challenge exists, but because it remains unacknowledged, unsupported or unresolved. When a challenge is carried silently, without space for reflection, repair or shared responsibility, its impact deepens.

In this way, addressing challenge is not simply about resilience or endurance, but about protecting leaders from the long-term erosion of purpose and wellbeing.

The challenge of culture: Inheriting, healing and rebuilding

Every leader inherits a culture.

Sometimes it's one you're proud to continue.

Sometimes it's one you need to gently realign.

Sometimes it's one you must completely rebuild.

Culture work is the most powerful work a leader can do and the most emotionally draining. Because, unlike policies, culture is not something you can simply 'fix'. It is lived, breathed and enacted by every single person in the school.

Culture is:

- How people speak to each other.
- How conflict is resolved.
- How behaviour is managed.
- How adults model expectations.
- How students feel when they walk into a corridor.
- How meetings start and how they end.
- How mistakes are treated.
- How success is celebrated.

Culture is the air people breathe at work.

Changing a culture, especially one wounded by mistrust, fear or inconsistency, is not a strategic exercise; it is a human one. Leaders often underestimate the emotional labour involved in restoring faith, rebuilding confidence and creating a sense of collective purpose.

Organisational research by Edgar Schein (2010) emphasises that culture is formed through 'repeated messages about what is truly valued'. That means your behaviour, more than your strategy, becomes the blueprint.

And here is the challenge most leaders don't see coming:

It is possible to change a policy overnight.

It is not possible to change a culture without changing hearts.

This is why authentic leadership matters.

People will commit to a vision only when they trust the person leading it.

The challenge of being 'The only One': Identity, expectation and representation

This is a challenge many leaders face, but few speak openly about, and it is one that resonates deeply with my own journey.

Being the only Black leader, the only woman, the only global majority colleague, or the only person with your lived experience in the room comes with a set of challenges that are invisible to those who have never carried them.

The McKinsey 'Women in the Workplace' report describes this as 'only-ness', a state where individuals feel hypervisible and invisible at the same time. Hypervisible because everyone sees you. Invisible because not everyone understands you (McKinsey, 2021).

For leaders of colour, the challenge isn't just to perform the role, it's to perform it flawlessly, because mistakes feel heavier, scrutiny feels sharper and the narrative around you can shift quickly. Many of us know the feeling of walking into a room and wondering:

- Will I be judged more harshly?
- Do I need to soften my tone?
- Will authenticity be welcomed or questioned?
- Do I carry the burden of representing everyone who looks like me?

When I was appointed as Headteacher at Copthall, it was soon after the appointment of a Black male Headteacher at an all-boys school just down the road. We had both inherited RI schools when all the others in the borough were either good or outstanding, and I recall years later when we were talking about our experiences, we both went back to 'remember when we were both appointed'. We both shared the same level of additional anxiety as new Heads because we were the only Black heads in the borough and we had been appointed to improve standards in RI schools, the pressure was immense and the fear of failing could have crippled us but we both went on to turn our schools around, we led with heart and authenticity but if we hadn't this is where imposter syndrome often creeps in, not because we doubt our ability, but because we are navigating institutions whose structures were not originally designed with us in mind.

But this challenge also holds power.

Representation is transformational.

When you show up authentically, you are not just leading, you are making space for others to follow.

What these challenges teach us: The quiet lessons leadership forces us to learn

The longer I led, the more I realised that challenges are not simply obstacles to overcome; they are teachers. They expose gaps, highlight blind spots, sharpen judgement and, whether we like it or not, force us to grow. They are uncomfortable lessons, but they are also the ones that stay with us long after the policy papers and action plans have been filed away.

Five quiet lessons I learned under pressure

Lesson 1: Clarity matters more than certainty

One of the hardest lessons is this: people do not need you to be perfect; they need you to be clear. Certainty is a luxury leaders rarely have. Clarity, however, is something we can offer every single day.

Clarity sounds like:

- This is what we know.
- This is what we don't know yet.
- Here's what we're doing next.

I reference the pandemic more than once because it was really a test of school leaders' resilience and ability to remain calm and authentic. We were often expected to operate with near-zero certainty. Staff didn't need a flawless plan; they needed clarity, reassurance and the confidence that we were anchored in our values, not the chaos.

Authentic leaders don't pretend to know the unknowable. They bring calm where others bring panic.

Lesson 2: Your values become your leadership North star

When the pressure is intense, it is easy, frighteningly easy to drift into reactive leadership. To do what will make the noise go away rather than what will make the culture healthier. But challenges expose what you truly believe.

Values-led leadership isn't a slogan; it's a discipline.

- *If you value kindness*, it must show in the hardest moments.
- *If you value equity*, it must show in recruitment, behaviour decisions and curriculum choices.
- *If you value transparency*, it must show even when the news isn't good.

- *If you value dignity*, it must show in difficult conversations, not just staff briefings.

  When you act from values, not pressure, people know.

  When you don't, people know that too.

Lesson 3: You cannot pour from an empty cup (despite trying)

Every leader has tried to be superhuman.

Every leader has paid the price for it.

The challenge here is that leadership burnout doesn't arrive dramatically; it creeps. It shows up as irritability, decision fatigue, loss of joy, poor sleep and that quiet sense of 'I used to handle this better'.

And, as the Education Support Wellbeing Index reminds us year after year, leaders consistently report the highest levels of stress across the profession, far higher than teachers.

Authentic leadership requires boundaries. Not because it is indulgent, but because it is responsible.

The truth is this: your school needs you well, not heroic. I know this is a hard one to balance, especially when the stakes are high, when scrutiny is relentless, and there will be days and possible periods of leadership when you are pouring from the bottom of your cup. It will be naïve for me to suggest this never happens; it does, but the key is for those moments to be far and few between.

Lesson 4: People will follow what you model, not what you announce

This is perhaps the most humbling challenge of leadership. Your staff do what you do, not what you say.

If you walk the corridors, they will walk the corridors.

If you meet problems with curiosity, they will meet problems with curiosity.

If you treat people with dignity, they will do the same.

If you panic, everyone panics.

Culture is contagious, for better or worse.

I've seen leaders try to 'install' new expectations while modelling the complete opposite. Staff see through it instantly. Authentic leadership demands alignment between your words and actions, *especially* when the challenge is high.

Lesson 5: Challenges reveal character: Yours and everyone else's

One thing I learnt, sometimes painfully, is that challenges expose who people really are.

Some colleagues rise, stepping forward with quiet leadership you would never have predicted.

Some retreat.

Some complain loudly while doing very little.

Some surprise you with their loyalty.

Some disappoint you with their behaviour.

But challenges also reveal *your* character.

Do you blame, or do you steady the ship?

Do you react, or do you reflect?

Do you protect others, or protect your ego?

Do you lead with compassion, or convenience?

It is rarely the big decisions that define you; it is the dozens of micro-decisions you make every day under pressure.

Four leadership moments that shaped me

I've always believed that leadership is not transformed by theories but by moments, small, significant moments that leave an imprint on how you show up. Here are four that stay with me.

Moment 1: The day I realised staff were watching me more than they were listening to me

Early in my headship, we had a whole-school briefing where I was trying to reassure staff during a turbulent period. I said all the right things, the words were polished, measured, hopeful. But afterwards, a member of staff quietly said to me:

> We heard what you said, but we were watching how you said it.

That moment knocked the breath out of me. I realised my tone, my body language and my presence were being analysed for clues. Leaders communicate with their whole selves, not just with words. It made me rethink everything, from how I entered a room to how I ended a necessary conversation.

Moment 2: The decision that cost me sleep but saved a child

Safeguarding challenges test your humanity more than your leadership. I once had to make a decision that I knew would deeply upset a family, create waves in the community and strain relationships. But it was the right decision for the child, and that had to be enough.

That challenge taught me that authentic leadership is not consensus-led. It is values-led. And sometimes you only sleep peacefully because you know you acted with integrity, not popularity.

Moment 3: The email that made me question whether I wanted to continue leading

Every leader has had *that* email, the one that is unfair, harsh, accusatory or deeply personal. The one that hits you at the wrong time, on the wrong day. I had one such moment where a parent criticised a decision I'd made to protect not just her child but the rest of the school community. Their words were unkind and inaccurate, but for a moment I questioned everything: my judgement, my resilience, my capacity to continue.

But after the tears dried, and the sting faded, I realised something: *Leadership doesn't break you, it shows you the parts of yourself that need strengthening.*

Not hardening.

Strengthening.

That email didn't end my leadership career.

It matured it.

Moment 4: The decision I made that I still carry with me

There is one leadership moment that shaped me more than I ever expected and one that still sits heavily on my heart even now. A year into my Headship, it was the day the Home Office contacted me to say they needed to come to the school to arrest one of our cleaners. A quiet, humble, elderly Ghanaian woman. Hardworking. Kind. The sort of person who brings warmth into a building simply by being in it.

She had overstayed her visa. The law was the law.

I remember the coldness of that phone call. The clinical language. The expectation that I would cooperate. And I did what the system required. I followed the process. I asked her to come to my office under the pretence that I needed to speak with her, but I made sure I wasn't there. Instead, the police were waiting.

I can still see her face.

Her confusion.

Her fear.

Her dignity.

She was arrested and later deported.

And even though I knew I had done what the law demanded, it felt like a betrayal. Not just of her, but of something deeper in myself, the belief that leadership is first and foremost about humanity. It was one of the toughest decisions I have ever made, and it changed me. Profoundly.

It taught me that leadership sometimes forces you into impossible spaces where every choice hurts, and where 'doing the right thing' legally can feel devastating morally. It made me understand, viscerally, the difference between compliance and justice. It also made me more determined to lead with compassion wherever I could, because I never wanted to feel that powerless again.

I will never fully forgive myself for that day.

But I also know it formed part of the leader I became, a leader who understands the weight of decisions that affect people's whole lives, not just their job descriptions.

And sometimes, that is the harshest challenge of leadership:

You live with the decisions long after everyone else has moved on.

The moral weight of leadership: When the right thing hurts

One of the realities we don't talk about enough in school leadership is the moral weight we carry. Not the strategic weight, not the accountability weight, the *moral* weight. The moments when you are required to make decisions that satisfy policy, law or safeguarding requirements, but break something inside you. These are the decisions the textbooks or an NPQ don't prepare you for.

Leadership often demands that you hold two truths at once:

- 'I did what was required' and
- 'I wish it could have been different'.

These dual truths can sit uncomfortably together, but they sit there nonetheless. And the challenge for authentic leaders is that we feel those moments deeply. We don't detach. We don't hide behind procedure. We don't switch off our humanity just because the situation is uncomfortable.

In fact, the more authentic and values-led you are, the more these moments shape you.

And this is why the phrase 'it's lonely at the top' isn't a cliché, it's a reality. Not because you lack people around you, but because you carry stories, decisions and consequences that you cannot always share. Some days, being a leader means managing the emotional fallout of decisions that were never really choices, just necessities.

This is the true challenge of leadership that few outside the role ever see: *the conflict between head, heart and responsibility.*

Leading through contradiction: When every path has a cost

If there is one thing guaranteed in school leadership, it's contradiction.

You are expected to be:

- Firm but empathetic.
- Strategic but present.
- Decisive but collaborative.
- Optimistic but realistic.
- Approachable but authoritative.
- Transparent but discreet.
- Available but not consumed.

In theory, these qualities sound balanced and reasonable.

In practice, they collide daily.

For example:

- Staff want consistency but also flexibility.
- Parents want fairness but also exceptions.
- Students want autonomy but also boundaries.
- Governors want ambition but also risk management.
- The system wants innovation but also compliance.

And you, as the leader, are expected to hold it all.

This constant negotiation is exhausting, not because you are doing anything wrong, but because you are doing everything expected. The challenge is to remain authentic when the pressures around you are pushing you into roles that do not feel natural.

What I learned, often the hard way, is this:

Authentic leadership is not about pleasing everyone.

It's about disappointing people at the right time, for the right reasons, with the right level of dignity.

Not everyone will like your decisions.

But they should always be able to understand them.

The challenge of capacity: When your to-do list doesn't match your humanity

One of the most relentless challenges leaders face is the mismatch between:

what the role demands and

what one human being is capable of.

On any given day, leaders can be expected to:

- Deal with a safeguarding disclosure before 9 am.
- Manage a behaviour incident by 10 am.
- Attend a strategic meeting at 11 am.
- Check in with a struggling colleague.
- Handle a parental concern.
- Respond to a DfE notification.
- Complete a return for the Trust or Local Authority.
- Observe teaching.
- Speak to students.
- Mediate a team disagreement.
- Solve a timetable issue.
- And still be inspirational, composed and available.

All before lunch.
And yet, leaders are often the last ones to admit:

'I'm stretched'.

'I'm tired'.

'I need help'.

Why? Because the culture of leadership still subtly or openly rewards endurance. I have worked in schools where leaders wore exhaustion like a badge of honour. 'I haven't had a day off sick in ten years'. 'I work until midnight'. 'I haven't seen my family all week'.

But authentic leadership rejects martyrdom.

Exhaustion is not a leadership strategy.

Capacity is not infinite.

And burnout doesn't just hurt leaders, it hurts the entire school.

The challenge is shifting from hero leadership to healthy leadership. Not easy, but essential.

The challenge of emotional labour: Caring without breaking

One of the most underestimated challenges in school leadership is emotional labour, the invisible work that comes with caring deeply, consistently and compassionately for others.

It looks like:

- Supporting a colleague who is grieving.
- Managing the emotions of a team after a traumatic event.
- Absorbing staff frustration while shielding them from external pressures.
- Holding space for children experiencing unthinkable things.
- Being the emotional buffer between competing pressures.
- Comforting a teacher who feels they have failed a student.
- Regulating your own emotions so you can help regulate those of others.

Leadership in schools is profoundly human work.

It demands empathy, patience, attunement and emotional intelligence day after day, sometimes hour after hour.

And the challenge is this:

How do you care without carrying everything?

Authentic leaders do not harden themselves; they learn to manage the emotional boundaries that protect both themselves and their teams. It took me years to realise that compassion does not mean absorption. You can care without carrying the full weight of everyone's emotions.

Emotional labour is invisible, but its impact is not. Leaders who ignore it burn out. Leaders who understand it create cultures where people feel safe, valued and understood.

Facing the challenges without losing yourself: A summative reflection

Another thing I have learnt from over two decades in leadership, it is this:

The challenges will never stop coming, but you can decide how you meet them.

Leadership is not defined by the absence of difficulty.

It is defined by the presence of integrity.

Every challenge, personal, professional, systemic, moral, leaves a mark. Some marks are painful. Some empower you. Some haunt you longer than you'd like to admit. But each one, without exception, shapes the leader you become.

- You will make decisions that keep you awake at night.
- You will carry stories that stay with you for years.
- You will hold the hopes and fears of others in your hands.
- You will lead through uncertainty, scrutiny, change and contradiction.
- You will sometimes do everything 'right' and still feel the weight of it all.

But here is what I know for certain:

You can face every challenge in this job without sacrificing your authenticity.

Your values are your anchor.

Your humanity is your strength.

Your integrity is your protection.

Your story is your compass.

The system may push you to harden, to perform, to comply or to lead in ways that do not feel like you. But authentic leadership is not about bending yourself into shapes that please others. It is about grounding yourself in who you are, consistently, courageously and compassionately, even when the landscape is uncertain.

And this is the ultimate truth of leadership challenges:

You cannot always control the storm, but you can control the leader you become inside it.

If authenticity is your core, you will not just survive leadership.

You will honour it.

Leadership reflection: Living with challenge

Leadership challenges are rarely experienced as isolated moments. More often, they accumulate quietly over time: decisions that linger, tensions that remain unresolved, responsibilities that sit heavily even after the working day has ended. This reflection is an invitation to acknowledge that reality, rather than push past it.

In leadership cultures that prize resilience, challenge is often framed as something to be endured, overcome or absorbed silently. While resilience is sometimes necessary, it can also become a burden when it discourages leaders from recognising the emotional and ethical impact of what they carry. Challenges do not only test competence; they test values, identity and capacity. Ignoring that cost does not make leaders stronger; it can make the work lonelier.

The questions that follow are not designed to catalogue failure or weakness. They are intended to create space for honesty. Authentic leadership requires more than staying the course; it requires knowing how challenge is shaping you, what it is revealing and what support might be needed to continue leading with integrity. Reflection allows leaders to process challenges rather than store them, reducing the risk that unresolved pressure hardens into withdrawal, cynicism or quiet burnout.

As you engage with these questions, notice where challenge has stretched you and where it may have depleted you. Pay attention to which experiences still carry emotional weight. This is not about dwelling on difficulty, but about recognising that leadership sustainability depends on making sense of challenge, not simply surviving it. Awareness is not an indulgence; it is a responsibility to yourself and to those you lead.

Take a moment to pause

Reflect on challenge and identity

- What is the hardest leadership challenge you have faced to date? What made it particularly difficult?
- Which challenge has stayed with you the longest, and why do you think that is?
- Have you ever felt pressure to lead in ways that did not feel true to who you are? What triggered that feeling?

Challenges often reveal not just what we face, but what we value.

Reflect on values under pressure

- Where have you had to choose between compliance and compassion? How did you navigate that tension?
- Which value or belief has anchored you most during difficult moments?
- Which challenges revealed your strengths, and what did they teach you

References

Bravata, D. M., Watts, S. A., Keefer, A. L., Madhusudhan, D. K., Taylor, K. T., Clark, D. M., Nelson, L. M., Cokley, K. O., & Haggerty, C. L. (2020). Prevalence, predictors, and treatment of impostor syndrome: A systematic review. *Journal of General Internal Medicine*, *35*(4), 1252–1275.

Clance, P. R., & Imes, S. A. (1978). The impostor phenomenon in high achieving women: Dynamics and therapeutic intervention. *Psychotherapy: Theory, Research & Practice*, *15*(3), 241–247.

Education Support. (2022). *Teacher Wellbeing Index 2022*. Education Support.

Education Support. (2023). *Teacher Wellbeing Index 2023*. Education Support.

McKinsey & Company. (2021). *Women in the Workplace*. McKinsey & Company.

NFER. (2023). *Teacher Labour Market in England Annual Report 2023*. National Foundation for Educational Research.

Schein, E. H. (2010). *Organizational Culture and Leadership* (4th ed.). Josssey-Bass.

12 Contributors

Authentic leadership in practice

Authentic leadership is often discussed as an idea, something to aspire to, refine or develop over time. But its real test is not theoretical. It is lived, shaped by context and revealed most clearly in moments of pressure, responsibility and choice.

Throughout this book, I have drawn on my own experiences of leadership to explore what authenticity looks like in practice, particularly when decisions are difficult, visibility is high and certainty is in short supply. But leadership is never exercised in isolation. It is influenced by the people we work alongside, the systems we navigate and the values we choose to uphold.

This chapter brings together the reflections of three leaders whose work has influenced, challenged and affirmed my own thinking. Each comes from a different context and leadership journey, yet all share a commitment to integrity, belonging and moral clarity. Their voices are not included to provide a single model of leadership, but to demonstrate how authenticity can take different forms while remaining grounded in shared principles.

What connects these reflections is not style or personality, but intent. Each leader speaks honestly about responsibility, identity and the quiet discipline required to lead with consistency. Together, they reinforce a central truth of this book: authentic leadership is not about being visible for the right reasons, but about being anchored when it matters most.

Elroy Aidouni-Cahill: Leading with conviction, kindness and courage

Elroy's leadership journey is shaped by his deep commitment to standards, belonging and recovery, particularly in contexts where trust must be rebuilt and expectations re-established. His reflections speak to the courage required to lead with clarity when systems are fragile and confidence is low.

What distinguishes Elroy's voice is his insistence that compassion and high standards are not opposites. He explores how leaders can protect dignity while

DOI: 10.4324/9781003635666-12

remaining uncompromising about expectations, and how belonging is strengthened, not weakened, by consistency and fairness.

Elroy's contribution reminds us that authentic leadership is not passive. It requires resolve, moral courage and the willingness to make decisions that may be uncomfortable in the short term but essential for long-term culture and trust.

Authenticity in leadership: Staying true to yourself

Elroy's leadership journey has been shaped by moments of clarity and conflict. 'I think I lost myself for a while', he reflects. 'I wasn't leading with heart. I wasn't sleeping easy at night with some decisions. And that's when I knew something had to change'.

He credits early mentors like Chris Mallaband for teaching him about moral leadership, about affecting change while staying true to your principles. 'Chris showed me you can be yourself and still do the right thing', Elroy says. 'And I think I'm a good person. I care about people. That's enough'.

Calling it out: Leading with integrity

Elroy shares candid examples of when he had to confront toxic cultures and unethical practices. At one school, he recalls suspending a member of staff and walking her off-site – not out of malice, but because her behaviour was 'so deeply destabilising' to the community. 'She had an axe to grind and had exhausted every possible avenue – unsuccessfully – but was determined to then make it personal. I'm not into gossip', he says. 'I'm into standards. The standard you walk by is the standard you accept'.

He's clear that authentic leadership means being willing to speak up, even when it's uncomfortable. 'If something doesn't sit right, you have to call it out. And if you're new in an organisation, you do it by listening first, then speaking with clarity and compassion'.

Creating belonging: Leading with kindness

One of Elroy's proudest moments was transforming Lift Kingsley, a secondary school in Hounslow, West London. Upon joining, the school had been judged as 'RI' twice in a row and was not on track to achieve a 'Good' grade at its next inspection. The school was on its fourth headteacher since opening, and had two deputies 'acting' up in the absence of a substantive head. Neither deputy got along with the other. 'The school was in this really sad limbo', he recalls, 'People were paralysed by not wanting to "take sides" with either deputy, and the school was just a deeply unhappy place'. Synonymous locally with 'dysfunction' and 'low standards'. Under his leadership, the school underwent a period of significant turnaround and achieved a 'Good' Ofsted rating, but more importantly, it became a place of belonging.

'We are together by circumstance, united by choice', he recalls, quoting a student. 'That sense of community, of care, that's what mattered most'. The school had lost its way, and despite superb staff and pupils, the sense of community was missing.

He led by example, teaching key exam classes, running interventions and walking the corridors. 'I wasn't going to ask anyone to do something I wouldn't do myself', he says. 'And the kids saw that I gave a damn. That's what made the difference. It was tough at times, I am not going to pretend that teaching an A Level group, and two GCSE classes, across three different subjects alongside being Headteacher was easy going, but it's important to "walk the talk"'.

Navigating identity: Finding space to be yourself

Elroy's journey has included navigating complex personal and cultural dynamics. He speaks thoughtfully about growing up in a context where being himself wasn't always easy. 'There was a lot of prejudice', he says. 'But being in England gave me more space to be me'.

He's found strength in being grounded in his values and in choosing how and when to share parts of his story. 'I've had to learn to be comfortable in my own skin', he says. 'And that's made me a better leader'.

Learning and evolving: Leadership as growth

Elroy credits his current experience working with Ele Lewis, Director of Strategy at Lift Schools, as transformative. In his new role, he supports schools and trusts that are considering joining the trust. 'It's the first time that I have had a direct line manager who has not come from the world of education. She's strategic, analytical and challenges me in the right way', he says. 'Importantly, she's not afraid to say when she's not sure about something, and will go and find out the answer. His attention to detail is second to none. It's been one of the most formative experiences of my career'.

He's learned to embrace purposeful challenge, to be open to feedback and to grow through discomfort. 'In schools, you can get defensive; it took me a while to adjust, and I am still learning', he admits. 'But I'm getting better at pausing, reflecting and adapting'.

Mistakes and setbacks: Lessons in resilience

Elroy is refreshingly honest about his mistakes. 'My first headship was a huge career mistake', he says. 'I feel like I had accepted the role, knowing that the fit wasn't right. The Trust was not in a great place and seemed to think that using a "cookie-cutter" approach was the right way to drive school improvement. But what works in rural Buckinghamshire is not necessarily going to work in urban Brixton', he recalls, 'I felt hampered, and couldn't lead change the way I wanted to'.

The leadership at the trust, at the time, was not operating in a way which matched his values, and he left without another job lined up, worried about how it would look. But he kept going, applying, reflecting and building a support network. 'Some feedback was rubbish, dressed up as valuable', he says. 'But I learned to be selective and to hold my nerve'.

He also reflects on being too quick to move people on in his first headship. 'I should have led improvement in a more measured way', he says. 'The second time around, at Lift Kingsley, I learned to bring people with me'.

Finding the right fit: Advice for aspiring leaders

Elroy's advice for aspiring leaders is clear: 'Listen to your gut. It's never wrong'. He urges leaders to do their research, talk to people and trust their instincts. 'While stability and time to prove impact are important, life's too short to stay somewhere that really doesn't feel right', he says. 'Don't be a martyr to your job'.

He shares a powerful reminder: 'When we pass on, our tombstone won't say "great employee". It'll say "loving family member". That's what matters'.

Inspiration: Leaders who made a difference

Elroy draws inspiration from a mix of personal connections and public figures:

- **Chris Mallaband, retired Headteacher at St Mark's CofE Academy in Mitcham** – 'The most formative influence on my career, he led with morals and great humour. I will never forget him telling me that the most important aspect of school improvement was "relentless positivity"'.
- **Ele Lewis, Director of Strategy at Lift Schools** – 'Strategic, thoughtful and a brilliant role model. Easily one of the most impressive leaders I have worked with'.
- **Becks Boomer-Clark, CEO at Lift Schools** – 'A really inspiring figure within the sector. She is fiercely unapologetic and wants more for the pupils we serve, and is constantly looking to innovate to raise standards. She is ambitious for young people, and unapologetically herself'.
- **George McMillan, Executive Headteacher and Assistant Director at Harris Federation** – 'I have never worked with him, but wish that I had and have followed his success from afar. He is quietly brilliant. I have heard of people travelling an hour and a half each way to work with him'.
- **Kiran Gill, CEO at The Difference** – 'Easily one of the most powerful influences in changing the narrative and advocating for a more inclusive system. Inspiring'.

- **Jacinda Ardern, Former Prime Minister of New Zealand** – 'Stepped back at the height of her career, when it was right for her personally and when she felt that someone else needed to take change forward. That takes real courage'.
- **Michael D. Higgins, President of Ireland** – 'Makes me proud to be Irish. He is bold, principled and doesn't give a damn'.

Sufian Sadiq: Leadership rooted in character, compassion and conviction

Sufian's reflections centre on character not as a performance, but as a daily practice. His leadership philosophy is rooted in humility, humanity and a strong sense of moral responsibility, expressed through what he describes simply as being 'a good egg'.

Rather than focusing on positional authority, Sufian speaks about the small, consistent choices leaders make and how these shape trust over time. His contribution challenges the idea that leadership requires dominance or visibility, instead highlighting the power of kindness, attentiveness and ethical steadiness.

Sufian's voice offers a powerful reminder that authentic leadership does not demand certainty in every moment, but it does demand integrity, especially when no one is watching.

Authentic leadership: Being a good egg

For Sufian Sadiq, authentic leadership begins with a simple but profound idea: *be a good egg*. It's a phrase he uses often in keynote talks, and it captures the essence of leading with integrity, humility and humanity.

He draws a compelling analogy from football. 'Some of the best players, Wayne Rooney, Steven Gerrard, Frank Lampard, were phenomenal on the pitch', he explains. 'But when placed in leadership roles, they didn't always succeed'. The same, he argues, happens in education: great teachers are often promoted into leadership without the emotional intelligence or relational depth needed to lead people well.

> In football, poor leaders get sacked. In education, poor leaders stay and teachers leave.

Sufian challenges the assumption that strong results equal strong leadership. 'You can achieve amazing outcomes and still fail your people', he says. 'Leadership isn't just about knowledge, it's about how you treat people'.

Cultivating trust: Leading with care

Sufian's approach to leadership is deeply relational. He shares a practical strategy: keeping notes on people he meets, details about their families, interests and lives. 'If someone tells me their child's name is Ali, I'll remember to ask how Ali's doing next time we meet', he says. 'That's how you show people you care'.

He recalls walking through a school with a newly appointed leader, brilliant in subject knowledge but struggling to connect.

> I asked him about the receptionist's daughter. He didn't know she was at the University of Bath, even though she talks about it all the time. That's the problem. If you don't invest in people, they won't give you their best.

For Sufian, authentic leadership is about effort, compassion and consistency. 'Relationships are the crux of humanity', he says. 'And you can't lead well if you don't care deeply'.

Navigating identity: Staying true to yourself

As a British Pakistani Muslim leader, Sufian speaks candidly about the tension between fitting in and staying true to who you are. 'There's a push-pull challenge', he says. 'Do I be who I am, or do I try to fit in?'

He reflects on the impact of Islamophobia and the pressure to code-switch in professional spaces. 'We didn't choose to stand out', he says. 'Sometimes you just wish you were like everyone else. But you have to remind yourself of your values, your heritage and your faith'.

Sufian's leadership is grounded in his belief that *work is worship*. 'Every interaction is an opportunity to live your values', he says. 'If I treat someone poorly, that's not worship. That's not who I want to be'.

He acknowledges the challenges of staying authentic in a system that often demands conformity. 'To be authentic, you need a reference point. You need values. And you need the courage to live by them'.

Leading with dignity: Compassion in difficult decisions

Sufian reflects on the complexities of school leadership, especially when it comes to managing underperformance. 'HR processes can suck the life out of what it means to be a good human', he says. 'We end up telling people they're not right for the profession, when really, they just weren't right for that school'.

He shares how he's learned to handle these situations with honesty and compassion. 'I'll say, "It's not working. Tell me how I can help you". I've moved teachers to different schools where they've flourished. You can end relationships with dignity'.

He warns against disingenuous support and microaggressions that erode trust. 'If you're secretly compiling a list of faults while ignoring others doing the same, that's not authentic. That's not being a good egg'.

Proud moments: Legacy through people

Sufian's proudest moments come from seeing those he's taught or trained become leaders themselves. 'There's a deputy head I trained, and an assistant head I taught as a student', he says. 'When people talk about them, they say, "He's such a gentleman. So kind. So positive". That's what makes me proud'.

He believes deeply in character over credentials. 'I'm not going to inspire someone with deep pedagogical theory', he says. 'But I hope I inspire them to live their values, to be good humans'.

He shares a powerful metaphor: 'Some of the greatest leaders in history were shepherds before they were prophets. They led from behind, with patience and care. That's the kind of leadership I believe in'.

Code-switching and community: Staying grounded

Sufian reflects on the experience of code-switching, adapting language and behaviour depending on the context. 'It's a protection mechanism', he says. 'But it's also a way to stay connected to our roots'.

He shares how his friends tease him when they see him speaking formally in public. 'They call me "Sebastian Sadiq"', he laughs. 'But I know I have to switch. I can't talk about inflation at the corner shop using words like "cognisant"'.

For Sufian, code-switching isn't inauthentic; it's a way to honour both his professional role and his community. 'I'm from the ends', he says. 'I've got friends who are Uber drivers, waiters, even in prison. I'm no different from them. I just got lucky'.

Inspiration: Leaders who stand for something

Sufian draws inspiration from a wide range of leaders:

- **Muhammad Ali** – 'He wasn't the best technically, but he believed in himself. That confidence is powerful'.
- **Imran Khan** – 'A leader who stood for the poor and the voiceless'.
- **Malcolm X** – 'A leader who stood for something'.
- **Chris Nicholls** – 'A college leader who cared more about people than results'.
- **Adrian Rogers and Lorraine Hughes** – 'Trust and backing are everything, especially for leaders from minoritised backgrounds'.
- **Dr. Patrice Evans** – 'A teacher who stayed true to herself and gave me confidence'.
- **Elif Ucar, his RE teacher** – 'She taught me character, not just curriculum'.
- **His parents** – 'They had a vision for us when we couldn't see it ourselves. That's leadership'.

Nav Sanghara: Leading with heart, heritage and humility

Nav brings a systems-aware lens to authentic leadership, focusing on alignment between values, behaviour and organisational structures. His reflections explore the importance of self-awareness, cultural intelligence and intentional decision-making, particularly in diverse and complex environments.

What stands out in Nav's contribution is his emphasis on coherence – between what leaders say, what they do and what they allow. He speaks candidly about the responsibility leaders carry to notice patterns, challenge inequity and ensure that values are not simply articulated, but enacted.

Nav's reflection reinforces the idea that authenticity is sustained not through individual intention alone, but through disciplined leadership that aligns values with systems, structures and everyday practice.

Authentic leadership: A journey of alignment

Nav Sanghara defines authentic leadership as a lifelong journey of aligning belief, behaviour and communication. 'It's values-first, people-centred and ego-last'. she says. Her leadership style is shaped by every relational transaction she's experienced, from childhood to the present day.

Growing up in a large Sikh family in South East London, Nav was immersed in a culture of service, community and shared joy. She recalls birthday traditions where cousins would open each other's gifts, and family members would feed one another cake, a symbolic act of care and connection. These early experiences instilled in her a deep sense of collective belonging and shaped her belief that leadership is about creating spaces where everyone feels seen and valued.

Standing firm: Values in action

Nav speaks candidly about moments when she's had to stand firm on her values, especially in high-stakes environments. 'There have been times when I've felt small in a dynamic', she reflects, 'but I've had to find that fire in my belly and speak up'. Whether challenging behaviour that misaligned with organisational values or navigating complex power dynamics, Nav has learned to trust her inner compass and act with conviction.

She emphasises that authentic leadership isn't about being loud, it's about knowing when to speak and when to observe. 'Not everything requires a challenge', she says. 'But if something keeps me up at night, I know I have to say something'.

Cultivating trust: From TA to CEO

Trust, for Nav, is built through relational connection. From her early days as a teaching assistant to her current role as CEO, she's relied on noticing, listening and following up. 'It's in every interaction', she explains. 'How you respond to an email, how you challenge someone, how you model decision-making'.

Starting her CEO role during the COVID-19 pandemic was particularly challenging. With staff appearing as 'little squares on a screen', she had to find new ways to connect. She leaned into her onscreen presence, held back-to-back virtual meetings and gathered stakeholder voices to understand the organisation's culture. 'I couldn't be in schools, but I could listen', she says. 'And that listening shaped everything'.

Vulnerability as strength

Nav shares how vulnerability has strengthened her leadership. 'People want to feel held and led', she says, 'but that doesn't mean you have to have all the answers'. During her transition into the CEO role, she leaned on friends, family and sector colleagues for support, something she hadn't done before. 'I embraced the not-knowing', she says. 'And that pause, that deliberation, became powerful'.

She recalls receiving feedback that she wasn't making decisions fast enough. But instead of reacting, she chose to reflect. 'I needed time to think. And later, people said it was powerful to watch me pause and be intentional'.

Navigating resistance and scepticism

Nav approaches resistance with empathy and curiosity. 'I am not my work', she says. 'If someone is sceptical, I try to understand what's going on for them'. She's learned to unpack emotions, avoid parent-child dynamics and hold adult-to-adult conversations that deepen understanding.

She shares a moment when someone asked, 'How do we know we can trust you?' Her response: 'I don't know. You'll have to decide that for yourself. But I'll always follow through on my values'.

Equity and fairness: Building systems that last

Nav believes fairness must be embedded in systems, not just intentions. 'Intent isn't enough', she says. 'We need policies, processes and structures that live out our values'. She's leading work on EDI and belonging across her trust, ensuring that equity is central – not an add-on.

She emphasises legacy: 'If I leave tomorrow, the organisation should still be fair and equitable. That's the gift we leave behind'.

Continuous growth: Leadership of self

Nav sees herself as a lifelong learner. Her growth is rooted in self-awareness, reflection and personal development. From coaching accreditation to breathwork and meditation, she invests in understanding herself so she can lead others with clarity and compassion.

'I've learned to calm my nervous system, to notice my triggers, and to use my gifts', she says. 'Leadership starts with the leadership of self'.

Identity and belonging: Showing up fully

As one of the few British South Asian female CEOs in education, Nav has navigated spaces where she's felt like the only one. Early in her career, she felt the need to 'switch on' at work and keep parts of herself hidden. But over time, she's embraced her full identity.

She shares a story about telling a colleague she was going to a Craig David pool party. Months later, that colleague said, 'It made me think I could be a headteacher too'. That moment unlocked something for Nav. 'People need to see that leadership is accessible', she says. 'I'm not special. I'm just me'.

Her father's story of coming to the United Kingdom at 17, working as a carpenter and eventually managing the Olympic Village project deeply inspires her. 'He taught me to work hard, be humble and be kind', she says. 'That's the fire in my belly'.

Inspiration and legacy

Nav's first leaders were her parents. Her mother modelled passionate leadership before it had a name, and her father showed quiet strength and connection. She's also inspired by Michelle Obama, sector colleagues and everyday interactions that leave her feeling lighter.

'Inspiration is everywhere', she says. 'But it's what you do with it that matters'.

13 Standing at the threshold

There comes a point in leadership when experience alone is no longer enough.

You may have the title, the track record, the credibility, even the confidence of others and yet still feel that something has shifted. The questions you are holding are no longer just about *what works*, but about *what matters*. Not simply how to lead, but who you are becoming as a leader, and what you are prepared to stand for when the answers are unclear.

For many leaders, this moment does not arrive with ceremony. It comes quietly, in a conversation that lingers longer than expected, in a decision that feels heavier than others. It can come after sitting in far too many leadership conferences, listening to how to balance a budget or manage difficult conversations and leaving with a heavier heart than when you arrived. It is the growing awareness that technical solutions no longer touch the complexity in front of you.

This is the threshold.

It is the space between what has been and what must now be shaped. A place where certainty gives way to judgement, and where leadership becomes less about control and more about responsibility. Standing here can feel uncomfortable. There are fewer guarantees. Fewer templates to follow. And far more scrutiny from others, and from yourself.

I often remind leaders that you are a Deputy Headteacher on 31st August and, almost overnight, on 1st September, you become the Headteacher. With that comes an unspoken expectation that you now have all the answers. You don't. Authentic leadership is not about becoming the person you once admired on a conference stage; it is about growing into the role as yourself. Anything else quickly becomes unsustainable.

Throughout this book, I have explored what authentic leadership looks like when it is tested: through challenge, visibility, belonging, values under pressure and the weight of the badge we carry. What becomes clear is that authentic leadership is not a destination you reach, but a practice you return to again and again, particularly at moments like this.

Standing at the threshold asks something specific of leaders. It asks you to slow down rather than rush to a resolution. To resist the pull of certainty when it comes

 DOI: 10.4324/9781003635666-13

at the expense of integrity. To recognise that leadership in complex times is less about having the right answer, and more about holding the right questions honestly, openly and with care.

This is not a call to hesitate or withdraw. It is a call to *choose*. To choose how you show up when the path ahead is not fully visible. To choose alignment over approval. And to choose to lead in ways that make it possible for others to trust, belong and remain even when the work is hard.

The chapters in this book have been about doing the work of authentic leadership. This final chapter is about living with it. About what it means to lead when the noise is loud, the context is fragile and the stakes for people, not just performance, are high.

If you are reading this and feel that you are standing at such a threshold, know this: you are not behind. You are not failing. You are being invited into the most meaningful phase of leadership, the one where values stop being aspirational and start becoming visible through action.

What authentic leadership demands (now)

There is a temptation, particularly in complex and pressurised systems, to reduce leadership to competence. To focus on what can be measured, managed and evidenced. But authentic leadership asks for more than capability. It asks for character.

What it demands *now* is not perfection, but clarity. Not certainty, but courage. Not visibility for its own sake, but consistency over time. These demands are not abstract; they show up in ordinary, often unremarkable moments, the meeting you choose not to rush, the behaviour you decide to challenge, the value you refuse to quietly compromise.

Authentic leadership demands courage, not in the dramatic sense, but in the quiet willingness to act when it would be easier to stay silent. Courage to name what is happening, even when doing so may make you unpopular. Courage to protect people's dignity, even when systems reward speed over care. This kind of courage rarely comes with applause, but it is noticed particularly by those who most need to feel safe.

It also demands *consistency*. Inconsistency erodes trust far more quickly than making the wrong call. Authentic leaders are not those who get everything right, but those whose decisions are grounded in recognisable values. Over time, people learn what you stand for, not because you announce it, but because your actions align with your words, even under pressure.

Authentic leadership demands clarity, especially when the context is ambiguous. This is not about having all the answers, but about being clear about what matters. When priorities compete, pressure mounts and values are tested, clarity becomes an act of leadership in itself. It reassures others that while the situation may be complex, the principles guiding decisions are not arbitrary.

One of the most testing periods in my career was during the pandemic. The responsibility of keeping everyone safe extended far beyond day-to-day safeguarding and into constant, high-stakes decision-making. There were moments when I believed it was safest to send whole classes, or even entire departments, home while simultaneously holding the responsibility of keeping the school open.

Guidance from the Department for Education was often unclear, and in that uncertainty, I realised that what staff and students needed most was not certainty, but direction. So I focused on providing that. I explained why decisions were being made, was honest about the judgement involved, and was clear that I was acting in what I believed to be the best interests of the community. I asked for trust and, crucially, I did so transparently. In time, that trust was given.

There is also a cost. Authentic leadership is rarely the path of least resistance. It can feel lonely. It may slow you down when others urge speed. It may require you to sit with discomfort rather than resolve it quickly. But it is this willingness to accept the cost rather than avoid it that sustains credibility over time.

It requires the discipline to keep returning to purpose. The humility to reflect and adjust. And the resolve to lead in ways that allow others to belong, contribute and trust, even when outcomes are uncertain.

These demands are not new. But in fragile systems, they become more visible. And they ask each leader the same quiet question: *What are you willing to hold steady when everything else feels in motion?*

Belonging as a leadership practice

Belonging does not happen by accident. It is shaped quietly and consistently by leadership choices.

Authentic leaders understand that people decide whether they belong long before they decide whether they will stay. Those decisions are rarely made in dramatic moments. They are formed in small, repeated experiences: how absence is noticed, how difference is handled, how mistakes are responded to, how welcome people feel when they return after difficulty. These moments tell people whether they are valued or merely present.

An all too familiar story I hear is from women who tell me, 'I've got to get out'. Not *I need to look for another job*, or *it's time for me to move on*, but *I need to get out*. Those words are visceral. They signal that something deeper is happening, that the culture and ethos of their setting have reached a point where they no longer feel they belong, and certainly no longer feel that they matter.

Often, the reasons come back to flexibility. Not a permanent request, not a lack of commitment, but a short period of adjustment while navigating caring responsibilities. Yet the response they receive is frequently framed around the inflexibility of the timetable, rather than a willingness to explore what *might* be possible.

As I grew as a Headteacher, I came to understand that small adjustments, or even the genuine attempt to make them, signal belonging. And when it simply wasn't possible to accommodate a request, explaining *why* still mattered. Clarity, once again, became the leadership act. It said: *you matter enough for me to try, and you matter enough for me to explain.* That, in itself, is how belonging is either strengthened or lost.

Belonging, therefore, requires leaders to be attentive, curious and willing to see their organisation from perspectives other than their own. This work is not always comfortable. Creating cultures of belonging often involves challenging established norms, questioning long-held practices and being open to feedback that may feel unsettling. It asks leaders to listen not in order to respond or defend, but in order to understand. To recognise when policies that appear fair on paper land unevenly in practice. And to act, even when doing so may be misunderstood or resisted.

Belonging also has a direct relationship with trust. In uncertain times, belonging becomes a stabilising force. When external pressures mount and confidence wavers, leaders cannot remove every challenge, but they can influence how safe people feel facing them together. Authentic leadership recognises that ensuring people feel they belong is not an optional extra; it is central to sustaining communities, retaining talent and protecting wellbeing.

Ultimately, belonging answers a simple but profound question for those we lead: *Do I matter here?* How leaders respond to that question through words, actions and decisions shapes not only culture, but futures.

Values under pressure

Values matter most when they are inconvenient.

In leadership, values are often expressed confidently in calm moments when options are plentiful, and consequences feel manageable. But authentic leadership is revealed under pressure, when decisions carry risk, when trade-offs are unavoidable and when the easiest option is not the right one.

Leading with values under pressure rarely feels comfortable. It often means choosing between competing goods rather than a clear right and wrong. Protecting dignity while holding boundaries. Acting in the best interests of the community while accepting that not everyone will agree. Authentic leaders understand that disagreement is not evidence of failure, but a natural consequence of principled leadership. For me, the key is not whether disagreement exists, but how it is handled. When it happens in private, grounded in evidence and communicated with clarity, that is the sweet spot of authentic leadership.

What sustains values in these moments is not rigidity, but intentionality. Leaders who lead authentically return repeatedly to their purpose, especially when decisions feel contested. They explain the reasoning behind their choices, acknowledge complexity and resist the temptation to hide behind policy or process alone. In doing so, they signal that values are not abandoned when circumstances become difficult.

Values under pressure also demand self-awareness. Stress can distort judgement and heighten emotional response. Authentic leadership involves recognising when pressure is shaping behaviour in unhelpful ways and creating space, however brief, to pause, reflect and seek perspective. This discipline protects values from being quietly eroded in the name of urgency.

Over time, it is this steadiness that builds trust. People may not always agree with the decisions made under pressure, but they are far more likely to accept them when they can see that values, not convenience or fear, were the guiding force. In this way, values become lived commitments rather than abstract ideals.

Authentic leadership does not promise comfort. It promises alignment. And when leadership feels most exposed, that alignment becomes the anchor for leaders themselves, and for those who look to them for direction.

This kind of leadership can feel lonely. Without clear right answers, leaders may carry doubt privately while projecting steadiness publicly. Yet it is precisely this steadiness, grounded in values and purpose, that allows others to feel secure enough to do their work, raise concerns and contribute honestly.

Ultimately, authentic leadership is not about predicting outcomes, but about shaping how uncertainty is held. When leaders act with integrity, explain their reasoning and remain accountable, they create conditions where trust can endure even when results are unclear.

There are no guarantees in leadership. But there is a choice, to lead with intention, courage and care in the face of uncertainty. And it is that choice, made repeatedly, that defines authentic leadership over time.

The invitation

This book does not end with answers. It ends with an invitation.

Throughout these chapters, I have explored what it means to lead authentically in schools, not as an abstract ideal, but as a daily practice shaped by pressure, people and context. Authentic leadership, as you will have seen, is not about having the right personality, the perfect strategy or the loudest voice in the room. It is about alignment. Between values and actions. Between words and behaviours. Between who you are and how you lead.

There will be days when leadership feels heavy. When decisions sit with you long after the meeting has ended. When progress feels slow, resistance feels personal and the responsibility you carry is invisible to others. Authentic leadership does not remove these realities. What it offers instead is a way of holding them with integrity, clarity and care.

This invitation is not to become a different kind of leader, but to become more fully yourself. To notice when you are acting out of fear rather than principle. To pause when certainty feels tempting but misaligned. To choose dignity, belonging and honesty even when they come at a cost.

You will not always get it right. No leader does. Authentic leadership allows space for reflection, repair and growth. It asks not for perfection, but for accountability. Not for certainty, but for steadiness. And not for control, but for trust.

As you move forward in your leadership journey, remember this: the impact of your leadership will not be measured only in outcomes, data or inspection judgements. It will be felt in quieter ways, in who stays, who speaks up, who feels safe enough to be themselves and who believes that they matter because of how they are treated in your presence.

Schools are built on relationships. Systems may shift, policies may change and pressures may intensify, but the human need to belong, to be seen and to be valued remains constant. Authentic leadership honours that truth.

So take this not as a conclusion, but as a beginning. A commitment to lead with intention. To hold your values steady under pressure. To create cultures where people can thrive, not despite the challenges, but because of how they are met.

The invitation is simple, but not easy:

Lead with clarity.

Lead with courage.

Lead with humanity.

And return to these choices, again and again, as you continue the work of authentic leadership.

Index

www.ingramcontent.com/pod-product-compliance
Lightning Source LLC
LaVergne TN
LVHW081738070826
845179LV00025B/339
9781041064893